VLADIMIR
ZHIRINOVSKY

The Man
Who Would Be
Gog

VLADIMIR ZHIRINOVSKY

The Man Who Would Be Gog

Scot Overbey

All scripture references are from the King James Version unless otherwise stated.

First Printing — March 1994 — 10,000 copies
Second Printing — April 1995 — 6,000 copies

Printed in the United States of America

Published by:
Hearthstone Publishing, Ltd.
500 Beacon Drive
Oklahoma City, OK 73127
(405) 787-4055 ● (800) 580-2604 ● FAX (405) 787-2589

ISBN 1-879366-74-6

TABLE OF CONTENTS

Chapter One

RUSSIA: GOD'S PROPHETIC BEAROMETER

Any student of Bible prophecy that is worth his salt and light can provide you with a quick list of prophetic people, places and events. These *"signs of the times"* lists can help serve as a barometer for us in the Christian life as we try to gauge the nearness of Christ's return and the end of the age. A list like this would typically include such items as:

1. The regathering of Israel—the fig tree of Matthew 24:32–35
2. A preponderance of false teachers and false christs (Matt. 24:5,11)
3. Wars and rumors of wars (Matt. 24:6)
4. Earthquakes in diverse places (Matt. 24:7)
5. Famine (Matt. 24:7)
6. Increase in lawlessness (Matt. 24:12)
7. Increase in knowledge and rapid travel (Dan. 12:4)
8. The Gospel will be preached to the whole world (Matt. 24:14)
9. The revived Roman Empire (Dan. 2:40-44; 7:7-8)
10. The Rapture of the Church (1 Thess. 4:16–17)
11. The rebuilt Temple in Jerusalem (2 Thess. 2:3–5)
12. The rise of Antichrist and the Abomination of Desolation (Matt. 24:15)
13. The Great Tribulation period (Matt. 24:21)

As helpful as these lists are, it seems they almost always fail to mention the prophetic events described in Ezekiel 38 and 39 involving the geopolitical area that we know today as Russia. As students of Bible prophecy, we must not forget that Russia is a very important BEARometer of God's prophetic plan for the ages. Let's look at the facts.

In Ezekiel 38 and 39 the Word of God says that in the last days there will be a massive invasion of Israel from the north. This last days assault on the nation of Israel will be led by a man that the Bible cryptically refers to as *"Gog."* The prophet Ezekiel goes on to tell us that this *"Gog"* is of the land of *"Magog"* and he is the *"prince of Rosh, Meschech and Tubal."* In Ezekiel 38:1–16 the Word of God says:

> *"And the word of the* LORD *came unto me, saying, Son of man, set thy face against Gog, the land of Magog, the chief (rosh) prince of Meshech and Tubal, and prophesy against him, And say, Thus saith the Lord* GOD; *Behold, I am against thee, O Gog, the chief prince of Meshech and Tubal: And I will turn thee back, and put hooks into thy jaws, and I will bring thee forth, and all thine army, horses and horsemen, all of them clothed with all sorts of armour, even a great company with bucklers and shields, all of them handling swords . . . After many days thou shalt be visited: in the latter years thou shalt come into the land that is brought back from the sword, and is gathered out of many people, against the mountains of Israel . . . Thou shalt ascend and come like a storm, thou shalt be like a cloud to cover the land, thou, and all thy bands, and many people with thee. Thus saith the Lord* GOD; *It shall also come to pass, that at the same time shall things come into thy mind, and thou shalt think an evil thought: And thou shalt say, I will*

go up to the land of unwalled villages; I will go to them that are at rest, that dwell safely, all of them dwelling without walls, and having neither bars nor gates, To take a spoil, and to take a prey . . . thou shalt come from thy place out of the north parts . . . And thou shalt come up against my people of Israel. . . ."

Most students of Bible prophecy are in agreement that this passage is referring to a last-days northern confederation of nations, led by Russia, that will storm southward into the Promised Land in an attempt to destroy Israel, plunder her wealth and take control of the Middle East. The present conditions in Russia make this event more likely than at anytime in recorded history. Russia is a starving, wounded bear, a mother bear robbed of her cubs. The present conditions in Russia have driven the once mighty Russian bear to the brink of despair and desperation. These brutal conditions are setting the stage for ultranationalist Vladimir Zhirinovsky to rise to power in Russia. However, before we take a detailed look at the present conditions in Russia and the rise of the man who would be Gog, we need to briefly consider Ezekiel 38 and 39. These two chapters contain a myriad of proper names that we need to be familiar with if we are to fully understand this passage (i.e., Gog, Magog, Rosh, Meshech, Tubal, Persia, Ethiopia, Put, Gomer, Beth-togarmah, etc.). However, for the purposes of this book, we will only focus on those dealing with Russia—Gog, Magog, and Rosh. Let's examine each of these proper names more closely.

LIFTING THE FOG AROUND GOG AND MAGOG

In Ezekiel 38:2 the Lord comes to Ezekiel and says, *"Son of man, set thy face against Gog, the land of Magog. . . ."*

After reading these verses, the person will ask two questions.

1. Who in the world is Gog?
2. Where in the world is the land of Magog?

These are great questions! Let's look at each one of these questions individually in order to once and for all cut through the fog surrounding Gog and Magog.

GETTING A GRIP ON GOG

First, the name Gog is a Hebrew word that literally means "high, supreme, a height, or a high mountain." When one examines Ezekiel's use of the name Gog in chapters 38 and 39, it seems quite clear that Ezekiel is referring to a person and not a place. For example, Ezekiel 38:2 says that Gog is of *"the land of Magog"* and that he is the *"prince of Rosh, Meshech and Tubal"* (NIV). It is apparent from Ezekiel's usage that Gog is a person from the land of Magog and he is the prince of the ancient peoples of Rosh, Meshech, and Tubal.

Many Bible scholars believe that the name Gog is best understood as a title rather than as an actual person's proper name. The fact that Gog means "high" or "supreme" makes this a likely possibility. If this is the case, Gog would be a kingly title, much like that of Pharaoh, Caesar, Herod, Czar, or President. It is interesting that this title is used eleven times by God in Ezekiel 38 and 39, thus making Gog the main character of the passage. Therefore, the Word of God clearly identifies Gog as the architect and driving force behind this massive end-times invasion of Israel.

Another indication that Gog is the name or title of a person is found in Ezekiel 38:15 and 39:2. Here the Bible clearly states that Gog is one who comes *"from the north parts."* Once again, Ezekiel's usage of the name Gog strongly indicates that it is the name or title of a person. According to

Ezekiel, Gog is one who makes his home in a region far to the north of the land of Israel. Ezekiel goes on to tell us that Gog, in a more specific sense, comes from the *"land of Magog."* Therefore, it is best to see Gog as a proper name or title. Now that we have established that Gog is the name or title of a person rather than the name of a place, let's move our attention to Magog.

MAPPING OUT MAGOG

Biblically speaking, the name Magog first appears in the table of nations of Genesis 10:2. Here the Bible tells us that Magog was one of the seven sons of Japheth (Noah's third son). Bible scholars tell us that after the flood, the descendants of Japheth settled all across the continent of Eurasia from the Black and Caspian Seas to Spain. It is interesting to note that the name Japheth means "enlargement," and in Genesis 9:27 the Bible says that Noah blessed the seed of Japheth and prayed, *"God shall enlarge Japheth."* Obviously, God answered this prayer as the descendants of Japheth have prospered and spread throughout the Eurasian continent. Therefore, in a broad general sense we can see that the descendants of Magog settled within the geographical area we know today as Eurasia.

As we have seen, the name Magog is also found in Ezekiel 38 and 39 where the Bible identifies the location of Magog as being in an area which is far to the north of Israel. Listen to the Word of God: *"And thou* [Gog of the land of Magog] *shalt come from thy place out of the north parts . . ."* (Ezek. 38:15). *"And I will turn thee* [Gog of the land of Magog] *back, and leave but the sixth part of thee, and will cause thee to come up from the north parts, and will bring thee upon the mountains of Israel"* (Ezek. 39:2).

It is apparent from the biblical references found in Genesis 10 and Ezekiel 38 and 39 that the land of Magog is linked to a person named Magog who was one of the seven sons of Japheth. Magog with the other descendants of Japheth are believed to be the original inhabitants of Eurasia. The Bible goes on to describe the land of Magog as being to the far north of Israel. Therefore, based on the biblical evidence alone, it is most likely that the land of Magog is equivalent to that area far to the north of the land of Israel that we know today as Russia and Central Asia. Central Asia includes the independent former Soviet republics of Kazakhstan, Turkmenistan, Tajikistan, Uzbekistan, and Kirghizia. Let's now turn our attention to the extra-biblical evidence pertaining to Magog.

One of the earliest extra-biblical references to the name Magog was made by Hesiod in the seventh century B.C. Hesiod is known as "the father of Greek didactic poetry." According to the writings of Hesiod, Magog was the father of an ancient group of people known as the Scythians. The Scythians were nomadic, marauding tribesmen from the Russian steppes who later settled in the fertile area of southern Russia just north of the Caucasus mountains and the Black Sea. It is interesting to note that the name Caucasus literally means "Gog's Fort."

The respected first century Jewish historian Josephus is in agreement with Hesiod's account. In his book *Antiquities*, Josephus has this to say about the identity of Magog: *"Magog founded the Magogians, thus they were named after him, but who by the Greeks are called the Scythians"* (*Antiquities* I, vi, i).

Like Hesiod, Josephus identified Magog as the land of the Scythians, the region north and northeast of the Black Sea and east of the Aral Sea. Josephus' explanation found acceptance with early Church fathers such as Jerome and Theodoret. The first century writer Philo was yet another ancient source who identified Magog with the Scythians and southern Russia. Also, Herodotus of Halicarnassus, known as the "Father of History," wrote about the Scythians as being descendants of Magog. According to Herodotus, the Scythians were a group of nomadic tribes who made their home in the area of the Russian steppes.

CONCLUSION

From this evidence it is clear that the land of Magog referred to in Ezekiel 38 and 39 is the ancient land of the descendants of Magog (Gen. 10:2). These descendants of Magog were also known as the Scythians. The Scythians were nomadic tribesmen who roamed the Russian steppes and later settled in the fertile area just north of the Caucasus mountains and the Black Sea. The homeland of the ancient Scythians is a geographical area that today includes parts of Russia, Ukraine, and also the Central Asian republics of Kazakhstan, Turkmenistan, Tajikistan, Uzbekistan, and Kirghizia. Therefore, the man who will be the Gog of Ezekiel 38 and 39 must emerge from this geographical area—the ancient land the Bible refers to as Magog.

IS ROSH REALLY RUSSIA?

In Ezekiel 38:2 the Word of God says: *"Son of man, set thy face against Gog, the land of Magog, the chief prince of Meshech and Tubal. . . ."* It is clear from this passage that Gog, who is of the land of Magog, will be the prince of Rosh. Is it really? The Hebrew word *rosh* literally means "top, sum, head, chief, or summit." The word rosh is quite common in the text of the Old Testament, where it is used some seven hundred and fifty times. Due to the general meaning of the word *rosh* and its frequency of use, many Bible translations prefer to translate the word rosh in Ezekiel 38:2 not as a proper name, but as a modifier of the word "prince." The translation would thus read as follows: *"Son of man, set your face toward Gog of the land of Magog, the chief prince of Meshech and Tubal. . . ."*

There is strong evidence to support this view. However, the more convincing evidence favors taking rosh as the proper name of a particular geographical place. The reasons are as follows.

First, many Hebrew scholars, including C.F. Keil and Wilhelm Gesenius, agree that the word rosh in Ezekiel 38:2 is used as a proper name for a specific geographical place.

Second, the Septuagint (the Greek translation of the Old Testament written just three hundred years after Ezekiel) translates the word rosh as a proper name.

Third, translating rosh as a geographical place is the most literal translation of the original Hebrew text. In fact, several well-respected translations of the Bible such as the New American Standard, the New English Bible, and the Jerusalem Bible translate rosh as a proper name.

Fourth, if Ezekiel were using rosh as a title in 38:2, then why isn't the title abbreviated when the phrase is repeated in 38:3 and 39:1? Normally, when titles are repeated in a passage they are abbreviated after the first occurrence. Based on these arguments it would seem that in Ezekiel 38 and 39, rosh is best understood as the proper name of a specific geographical place.

If rosh is best interpreted as being a proper name for a geographical location, the next logical question to ask is: Where is rosh located? Does rosh refer to Russia? In Ezekiel 38:15 and 39:2 the prophet links rosh militarily and geographically with other nations who will come to invade Israel from the "remote parts of the north." While this is helpful information, it does not provide us with any specificity regarding the precise location of rosh. Once again, a study of ancient history and extra-biblical sources is helpful.

Ancient history reveals that rosh in Ezekiel's day was composed of a group of fierce northerly people called the Sarmatians. The Sarmatians were a nomadic people that traveled around the area of the Caspian Sea beginning in approximately 900 B.C. The ancient Assyrians referred to the Sarmatians as the *Ras* or *Rashu*. In fact, one ancient Assyrian inscription, dated around 700 B.C., refers to an attack on the Ras in the land of Rashu. The ancient Assyrian reference to the land of Rashu and the Babylonian equivalent, *Rasapu,* is best identified with the Sarmatians who inhabited the area around the Caucasus Mountains between the Black and Caspian Seas. Herodotus confirms this location in Book Four of his *Histories.* In his writings, Herodotus describes Sarmatia as being between the Black and Caspian Seas just north of the Caucasus Mountains. This area today includes parts of Ukraine, southern Russia, and the former Soviet republics of Armenia, Georgia, and Azerbaijan.

The respected Hebrew scholar, Wilhelm Gesenius, says this about rosh: *"Rosh is undoubtedly a reference to the Russians, who are mentioned by the Byzantine writers of the tenth century, under the name Ros, dwelling to the north of Taurus . . . as dwelling in the river Rha (Wolga)."*

Also the words *Rus* and *Ros* were used as the names of the great Kievan Empire (A.D. 862). Eventually, they became the name of the entire area that we know today as Russia when the Latin prefix *"ia"* was added sometime during the sixteenth century. Therefore, one can make a strong argument from the historical evidence that rosh is indeed Russia!

THE STAGE IS SET

It is clear from our brief study that the events described in

Ezekiel 38 and 39 involve the Russian bear. Therefore, Russia should be kept in the forefront of the mind of every serious student of Bible prophecy. Russia is most definitely a **bear**ometer of God's prophetic program for the ages.

Today, Russia is a nation in crisis! Hyperinflation, rising crime, political instability, and a badly bruised national ego due to the dissolution of the Soviet Empire have brought the once-mighty Russian bear to the point of desperation and despair.

I believe very strongly that the current conditions in Russia are setting the stage for the rise of a powerful leader like Gog of Ezekiel 38 and 39. The Bible tells us three main facts about Gog.

First, the Bible tells us that Gog will emerge out of the land of Magog. As we have seen, the ancient land of Magog includes parts of modern-day Russia, Ukraine, as well as the Central Asian republics of Kazakhstan, Turkmenistan, Tajikistan, Uzbekistan, and Kirghizia.

Second, the Bible tells us that Gog will be the prince of rosh. As we have noted, the Hebrew word rosh is best translated as a proper noun referring to a particular geographic place. Both biblical and extra-biblical evidence alike indicates quite conclusively that rosh is equivalent to the geopolitical area we know today as Russia.

Third, the Bible tells us that in the last days, Gog will lead a powerful confederation of nations in a massive invasion of the land of Israel.

WHAT IS THE POINT?

The premise of this book is that the Gog of Ezekiel 38 and 39 may already be on the world scene right now! This *"man who would be Gog"* is none other than Russian ultranationalist Vladimir Volfovich Zhirinovsky, who is the fastest rising political star in Russia today.

Amazingly, Zhirinovsky fits Ezekiel's description of Gog to the letter. First, Zhirinovsky was born in Alma-Ata, Khazakhstan. As we have seen, the Central Asian republic of Khazakhstan is situated comfortably within the boundaries of the ancient land that the Bible refers to as Magog. Therefore, Zhirinovsky, like Gog, is from the land of Magog.

Second, Zhirinovsky has positioned himself very favorably to become the next president of Russia. In Russia's December 12, 1993 parliamentary elections, Zhirinovsky's Liberal Democratic Party received more votes than any other political party. If Zhirinovsky is successful in his quest for Russia's top political prize he, like Gog, will instantly inherit the biblical title, "prince of Rosh."

But most intriguing of all is Zhirinovsky's unabashed desire to lead Russia on her final military push to the south. In his recently published autobiography which is apocalyptically entitled, *Last Dash to the South*, Vladimir Zhirinovsky makes the following statements which sound as if they could have been taken straight from the pages of Ezekiel 38 and 39.

*"A great **historical** mission has fallen to Russia. **It may be its last.** So, the idea emerged of the last 'dash'–last because it will probably be **the last repartition of the world** and it **must be carried out in a state of shock therapy—suddenly, swiftly, and effectively.** The last dash to the south, Russia's outlet to the shores of the Indian Ocean and **Mediterranean Sea.** Russia must therefore go south and reach the shores of the Indian Ocean. This is not just my whim. **It is Russia's destiny. It is a fate. It is Russia's great exploit.** We must do it, because we have no choice. There is no other way for us. It is geopolitics. Our development demands it, like a child who has out-*

*grown his clothes and must put on new ones. Let Russia successfully accomplish its last dash to the south. I see Russian soldiers gathering for this last southern campaign. I see Russian commanding officers in the headquarters of Russian divisions and armies, sketching the lines of march of troop formations and the end points of their marches. I see planes at air bases in the southern districts of Russia. I see submarines surfacing off the shores of the Indian Ocean and landing craft approaching the shores, where soldiers of the Russian Army are already marching, infantry combat vehicles are advancing and vast numbers of tanks are on the move. **Russia is at last accomplishing its final military campaign.** "*

CONCLUSION

Could it be that Vladimir Zhirinovsky is the power-crazed leader that the Bible says will one day lead Russia and a host of other nations south to invade Israel? Is Vladimir Zhirinovsky the man who would be Gog? As we will see in the coming chapters, the evidence is most compelling. Let's take a closer look at the man himself and the conditions that have propelled him into the international spotlight.

Chapter Two

IN THE BEGINNING GOG

In his autobiography, *Last Dash to the South*, which also serves as his political manifesto, Vladimir Zhirinovsky describes his childhood as one of:

1. Constant hunger—*"All my childhood memories are associated with the fact that I never had enough to eat."*
2. Stark economic deprivation—*"My whole life was poverty, I never had money for anything."*
3. Misery—*"Life itself forced me to suffer from the very day, the moment, the instant of my birth. Society could give me nothing."*

This book, which Library of Congress historian James Billington calls *"a more psychologically unstable work than Hitler's* Mein Kampf,*"* is full of detailed experiences that help shape the deeply resentful and dark personality of Vladimir Zhirinovsky.

THE NAME GAME

Vladimir Volfovich Zhirinovsky was born April 25, 1946. It is interesting to note that the Russian name *Vladimir* literally means "master of the world." This is a very appropriate name, because as we will see from Zhirinovsky's own writings, he unabashedly declares his intent to raise Russia to a position of world dominance by the use of military force.

Sergei Grigoriantz, a Russian Jew reporting for the *Jerusalem Post* on January 29, 1994, says this:

> *"The West does not understand the mentality of people like Zhirinovsky. The West does not take his territorial ambitions seriously. If Zhirinovsky comes to power he will begin a war to gain territory, and there will be a threat to the entire civilized world."*

Master of the world indeed!

Vladimir Zhirinovsky's middle name is Volfovich. The name *Volfovich* literally means "son of a wild canine." Ariel Cohen, an expert in Russian and Eurasian studies with the Heritage Foundation, writing for Knight-Ridder on December 27, 1993, says this:

> *"Zhirinovsky's statements indicate an evil and an ambition unknown even in the animal kingdom. Zhirinovsky means carnage for Russia and her neighbors."*

READY OR NOT, HERE I COME

Zhirinovsky's entrance into the world was not without incident. In his autobiography, Zhirinovsky describes that the maternity ambulance did not reach his mother in time to take her to the hospital, therefore his mother was forced to deliver him in the one-bedroom apartment where they lived. Zhirinovsky feels that he himself somehow initiated the timing of his birth due to the importance of his life mission:

> *"I was born right there in the apartment, in the very room where I spent the next eighteen years of my life. . . . Maybe this moment of birth had some kind of effect on my future fate? Maybe I myself provoked it somehow. I could not wait."*

From statements like this, it is clear that Zhirinovsky sees himself as a man of destiny—a man with a world-changing life mission.

WRONG JIDE OF THE TRACKJ

Oddly enough, Zhirinovsky, who is the consummate Russian ultranationalist, was himself not born in Russia. Rather, he was born in Alma-Ata, capital of what was then the Soviet republic of Khazakhstan. Khazakhstan is a Central Asian republic which has since declared its independence from what was the Soviet Union. To this day, Zhirinovsky remains very sensitive about his place of birth and its current non-Russian status.

> *"Russian people founded this city. So I am always entitled to consider that I was born in Russia among Russians. It is idiotism that my birthplace and the place of my grandmother's burial, might be considered a foreign country for a Russian. It was Russia who brought cities and subways and industry to distant undeveloped places such as Kazakhstan."*

HITLER YOUTH

Vladimir was the youngest of six children born to Volf and Alexandra Zhirinovsky. Zhirinovsky's mother was a Russian, but his father was apparently a Polish Jew by origin. His father died in a car accident when Zhirinovsky was still an infant. Soon afterward, Zhirinovsky's mother was forced to take a job cleaning a local cafeteria in order to provide food for him and his five older brothers and sisters. Zhirinovsky recalls:

> *"All my food came from the cafeteria. It was re-*

volting food, of course, and it naturally wrecked my digestion and promoted the development of gastritis, cholecystitis, and so forth. But what could I, a small boy, do? I was always hungry."

At the age of two or three, Zhirinovsky recalls how he was sent by his mother to live-in child care. Zhirinovsky still remembers that each night the children would be awakened at eleven P.M. by the staff and lined up naked—boys and girls in the same room—to urinate in buckets.

"I spent six days a week in a room with twenty-six beds and twelve little kids. I remember that nursery to this day. We were put to bed at nine, then wakened at eleven. They would wake the whole group, put two buckets in the middle of the room, and switch on the light. Boys would urinate in one bucket, girls in the other."

In his autobiography, Zhirinovsky shares a very detailed account of his first eighteen years. It is an extremely sad story of poverty, rejection, and loneliness which can best be summed up in the following quote:

"So even from childhood I felt somehow uncomfortable and unpleasant. I was deprived of the most basic family comfort and human warmth. It was a joyless childhood all eighteen years."

In his autobiography, Zhirinovsky (like Hitler) admits that his extreme political views find their origin in the intense anger and resentment that he felt concerning his early childhood experiences. One particularly vivid recollection that Zhirinovsky shares is the time he asked his mother why their family had such bad housing conditions in Alma-Ata. Apparently, they were forced to share a small communal apartment space with other families. Zhirinovsky's mother replied,

> *"We're not Kazakhs. It is very difficult for us to get an apartment here because we are Russians and the Kazakhs are given preference."*

With stories like this, it is no wonder that Zhirinovsky has been able to endear himself to some twenty-five million Russians who currently reside in newly-independent former Soviet republics like Kazakhstan.

LOOKING FOR LOVE IN ALL THE WRONG PLACES

At age eighteen, with nothing but a small satchel and a basket filled with an assortment of tomatoes and strawberries, Zhirinovsky moved to Moscow where he enrolled at the Institute of Oriental Languages (also known as the Institute of Asian and African Countries, and as a favorite training ground for the KGB) at Moscow State University. While there, Zhirinovsky majored in Turkish. Later, Zhirinovsky would earn his law degree from the same institution. Although a good student, Zhirinovsky had little success making close friends, especially those of the opposite sex. Sadly, Zhirinovsky admits that he has never had a true love or even a real friend. In fact, Zhirinovsky confesses that he has never even felt real passion for his wife or son.

> *"At the age of twenty when a young man ought to be falling head-over-heels in love and dating girls, I was sitting at my studies. And later on, when I was twenty-four, it was not the same, something had burned out. I had somehow missed out on this particularly early surge of lyricism of love, there was nobody to set me on the right road. This naturally*

impoverished my heart. As a result I never fell in love with anyone. And throughout my later life, I have never met the woman I need, the woman I can love. Clearly, this was my fate, never really to experience anything of either love or friendship. I have never been deeply in love with my wife. Our personal relationship has been okay, but we have not been head-over-heels in love. The same goes for my attitude toward my son."

From a statement like this it is clear that Vladimir Zhirinovsky is a monomaniac with a mission. His one over-riding passion is to see his geopolitical aspirations for Russia become a reality. According to Zhirinovsky, *"This is the juice of my brain."*

I ƧPY

Upon graduation from the Institute of Oriental Languages in 1969, Zhirinovsky went to Turkey to serve first as a low-level Soviet translator, then as a mid-level cultural liaison, and later, as a top Russian trade official. To many, Zhirinovsky's quick rise through the ranks of the Soviet bureaucracy is cause for suspicion. According to Jack Anderson, the fact that Zhirinovsky was allowed to work abroad in the '70s after college, especially in a NATO-member country like Turkey, would have required KGB permission at a minimum.Some experts believe that these assignments were jobs typically used as cover for KGB agents who would be posted abroad. However, Zhirinovsky vehemently denies that he was ever a card-carrying member of the Communist Party or a KGB operative. In fact, Zhirinovsky has filed numerous libel suits in Moscow against those who have said otherwise.

While serving in Turkey, Zhirinovsky was arrested for distributing Soviet lapel pins and badges, which the Turkish government considered to be propaganda. Those close to Zhirinovsky believe that this rather embarrassing incident may be one of the main reasons he never was accepted into the Communist Party.

YOU'RE IN THE ARMY NOW!

During the years 1970–72, Zhirinovsky served as a staff specialist in the Transcaucasus Military District Staff Political Directorate. Zhirinovsky was stationed in Tbilisi, Georgia. While in Georgia, Zhirinovsky received special training in the areas of army intelligence and special propaganda. It was at this time that Zhirinovsky got to know the army itself. Zhirinovsky was able to travel extensively in Georgia, Armenia, and Azerbaijan. During this period he became known as a specialist on problems of Central Asia, the Transcaucasus, and the Near East. It was also during this period that Zhirinovsky undertook what he called *"a deeper study of the nationalities problem."* It was no doubt at this time that Zhirinovsky first began to develop his geopolitical vision which he would later code name *Last Dash to the South.* Zhirinovsky's study of the "nationalities problem" led him to the following conclusion:

> *"All Russia's problems are in the south. So until we resolve our southern problem, we will never extricate ourselves from the protracted crisis, which will periodically worsen."*

REJUME OF V.V. ZHIRINOVJKY

The remaining details about Zhirinovsky's past are somewhat sketchy. In fact, one reporter commented that Zhirinovsky's past has more holes than Russian cement.

Therefore, let's examine them in summary fashion.

1970s—After receiving his law degree, Zhirinovsky goes to work for Inyurkollegia, an association of lawyers specializing in international cases. Zhirinovsky leaves under a cloud of bribery allegations.

1983–1990—Zhirinovsky heads legal department of Mir (Peace), a publishing house. Works for Soviet Peace Committee and a pro-Jewish organization known as Shalom, both of which were government sponsored.

December 1989—Zhirinovsky helps found the Liberal Democratic Party. It is interesting to note that at this time, any non-communist political party that wanted to obtain official legal status could expect to face a myriad of difficult roadblocks. However, Zhirinovsky's party seemed to have little difficulty. The Liberal Democratic Party was organized and licensed without any problems.

March 1990—Zhirinovsky takes control of the Liberal Democratic Party, first non-communist political party in Soviet Union.

June 1991—Zhirinovsky runs for president

and finishes third, behind Boris Yeltsin and Nikolai Ryzhkov.

August 1991—Zhirinovsky supports the failed coup against Mikhail Gorbachev.

December 12, 1993—Zhirinovsky is elected to Russian parliament. His Liberal Democratic Party shocks the world by receiving twenty-five percent of the votes cast (more than any other party).

From this history, it is clear that, educationally, philosophically, militarily, linguistically, legally, politically, geographically—anyway you slice it—Vladimir Zhirinovsky has the perfect resume for the man who would be Gog.

THE JEWISH CONNECTION

Rumors abound concerning the reported Jewish connection in Vladimir Zhirinovsky's past. Could it be that Zhirinovsky, the Russian supernationalist who once blamed the Jews for two world wars and who is known for his inflammatory anti-Semitic rhetoric—could it be that he himself is the son of a Polish Jew?

Stories about Zhirinovsky's Jewish roots have been circulating ever since he helped found the Liberal Democratic Party in 1989. In his autobiography, *Last Dash to the South*, Zhirinovsky simply sidesteps the question of his lineage by saying that his mother was Russian and his father was a lawyer named Volf (this would be a very unusual name for a Russian).

Following his victory in the December 1993 parliamentary elections, Zhirinovsky was questioned repeatedly by reporters concerning whether his father was indeed Jewish, to which Zhirinovsky heatedly replied: *"Never, never; my mother is Russian, my son is Russian . . . only Russian. All my family is Russian."*

The Moscow *Kuranty* reported that while attending the December 12, 1993, Russian election-night gala, a triumphant Zhirinovsky ran into Armenian-born democrat Telman Gdlyan, whose New Russia Bloc Party could not get on the ballot. Upon seeing his political rival, Zhirinovsky guffawed, *"So, when are they going to make you commander of the Armenian army?" "The same day they make you commander of the Jewish army,"* Gdlyan responded. Zhirinovsky slugged him. The *Kuranty* reported that Gdlyan was about to strike back when a group of Zhirinovsky's bullish young bodyguards blocked his way.

Needless to say, the question of a Jewish bloodline makes the blood of Vladimir Zhirinovsky boil red-hot. One former colleague who knew Zhirinovsky for several years while the two worked together at the Foreign Judicial Collegium (a government group that provided legal assistance for Soviet citizens in foreign countries) said that Zhirinovsky was indeed regarded as a Jew by his co-workers, but that they never discriminated against him because of that. Of course, Zhirinovsky was quick to deny these reports saying, *"This was a dirty slanderous lie."*

A reporter working for the Associated Press and Cable News Network recently discovered public records which seem to prove Zhirinovsky's Jewish connection.

"Public records show that Vladimir Zhirinovsky, the Russian nationalist leader who campaigns on anti-Semitic themes, had a Jewish last name until age 18. Zhirinovsky's origins have political significance in Russia because of his criticism of Jews, and the docu-

ments raise questions about his candor. . . . Although the records do not say specifically who his father was, Zhirinovsky's surname was listed on his birth registration as Eidelshtein. Documents show he applied for and received permission to change his name from Eidelshtein to Zhirinovsky in June 1964 (just before he moved to Moscow from Kazakhstan). The worn, handwritten documents at the Alma-Ata archives were retrieved from dusty shelves and cardboard boxes in response to a reporter's inquiries. Officials at the archives said the documents were authentic. In his autobiography, Zhirinovsky claims his father was named Volf Fudreyevich Zhirinovsky, but no records could be found for such a man in Alma-Ata. Details about the father in the autobiography seem to combine elements from his mother's two husbands. One husband was Andrei Vasilyevich Zhirinovsky, who died of tuberculosis in August 1944, eighteen months before Zhirinovsky's birth on April 25, 1946. A marriage registration shows that five months before Zhirinovsky was born, his mother married Volf Isakovich Eidelshtein, who was officially listed as a Jew. There is no further record of Eidelshtein."

Once again Zhirinovsky is quick to deny these reports. Zhirinovsky told CNN News in an interview that these documents had been "prepared against me," possibly by Russian security agents.

Zhirinovsky is constantly sending out mixed signals with regard to his Jewish sentiments. One moment he will sound like the "Russian Hitler"; the next moment he will sound like a sympathetic friend of the Jew. In a December 17, 1993 Associated Press article, Mikhail Gendelev, a poet and journalist who interviewed Zhirinovsky for a Russian-language newspaper published in Israel, was quoted as saying this about Zhirinovsky's Jewish sentiments:

> *"He [Zhirinovsky] told me: 'Let us [Russia] deal with the Turks and Iran first, then we will carry out territorial exchange and lift the Arab world's pressure off you.' He suggested giving the Arabs another piece of land, instead of Israel—at the expense of Iran and Turkey."*

Along the same line, Israeli officials disclosed that in 1983 Zhirinovsky was granted permission to emigrate to Israel, an invitation that normally requires proof of Jewish background. Also in the 1980s there was the mysterious involvement by Zhirinovsky with a group called *Shalom*, an outwardly pro-Jewish organization. Although it would appear from these reports that Zhirinovsky is at times sympathetic to the Jewish cause and possibly even desiring to emigrate to Israel himself . . . nothing could be further from the truth.

One doesn't have to listen to Zhirinovsky for very long to discover that he is strongly anti-Semitic. In fact, Zhirinovsky is so anti-Semitic that he is being called "the Russian Hitler," and was even refused entry by Germany on a recent European trip. Zhirinovsky constantly blames foreigners for Russia's decline, more often than not warning of a Zionist plot. Also, Zhirinovsky's Liberal Democratic Party has received large amounts of financial support from a Russian organization called *Pamyat*. *Pamyat* is the largest and strongest of Russia's anti-Semitic groups. According to Ann Simmons in *Time* magazine (Jan. 13, 1992):

> *"Russians are looking for someone to blame for the shortages and hunger that have followed the collapse of communism, and many are finding that all-purpose, historic scapegoat, the Jew. In Russia, the*

umbrella organization for this type of hatred is a group known as Pamyat, *which preaches a sacred Russian nationalism looking toward an authoritarian Russia purged of all foreign influences. The leader of one such group is Vladimir Zhirinovsky. . . ."*

Let's take a closer look at some examples of Zhirinovsky's anti-Semitic rhetoric.

"Although my party is not anti-Semitic, we don't tolerate an increase in the strength of the Jews."

"I will replace all of Moscow's Jewish television announcers with blue-eyed Russians."

"Jews are infecting the nation!"

"The Jews were to blame for the first two world wars, and it is they themselves who have provoked anti-Semitism."

"In Russia today, Jewish children are going to school while our children are hungry and forlorn. If you elect me I will put a stop to it."

"I myself am not an anti-Semite, but the best outcome would be for a free emigration of Jews out of Russia to Israel. It would be best if they would all go back to Israel."

"Whenever I am bashed in the press, the article is usually signed by a Jewish name."

"The majority of the new political parties, unfortunately, are headed by Jews, and a Russian Jew is against Russia, because there was anti-Semitism in our country and still is. But we [the Liberal Democratic Party] are not anti-Semitic."

With talk like this, it is no wonder that concern among Russian Jews is rising. Jewish pessimism about Russia's future has increased dramatically since the December 12, 1993 elections in which Zhirinovsky's Liberal Democratic Party won twenty-five percent of the popular vote. The number of Jews deciding to emigrate is on the rise. Rabbi Pinchas Goldschmidt, the chief rabbi of Moscow says:

> *"The recent rise of extreme nationalism in Russia due to the economic situation gives us reason enough to believe that the next president of Russia will be a member of today's opposition. Zhirinovsky or another like him. Therefore, Jews must prepare themselves for the 1996 presidential elections, when Mr. Zhirinovsky or someone else in the opposition might prevail. We must hope for the best but prepare for the worst. . . . I'm the last person among Jews in this country to say it but, I fear that in the long term there is no future for the Jew here. I think we must begin to prepare our children for lives outside Russia"* (*New York Times*, 2/5/94).

CONCLUSION

The Bible says in Ezekiel 38 and 39 that in the end times a power-crazed ruler referred to as "Gog" will lead a massive Russian invasion into Israel. This man, like Zhirinovsky, will be an anti-Semite with a desire to conquer and plunder Israel. In Ezekiel 38:8-13 the Word of God declares:

> *"After many days thou shalt be visited: in the latter years thou shalt come into the land that is brought back from the sword, and is gathered out of many people, against the mountains of Israel . . . Thou shalt ascend and come like a storm, thou shalt be like a*

cloud to cover the land, thou, and all thy bands, and many people with thee. Thus saith the Lord GOD; *It shall also come to pass, that at the same time shall things come into thy mind, and thou shalt think an evil thought: And thou shalt say, I will go up to the land of unwalled villages . . . To take a spoil, and to take a prey . . . to carry away silver and gold, to take away cattle and goods, to take a great spoil.*"

Interestingly, Zhirinovsky, just like Ezekiel's Gog, sees Israel as a nation of tremendous wealth. Listen to the following quote from this man who could be Gog: *"I envy the Jews because they are the richest nation in the world!"*

Talk of Jewish ancestry is not the only mysterious rumor swirling around Vladimir Zhirinovsky. There is also much speculation about a possible link between Zhirinovsky and the KGB.

KaGey Bear

The success of Vladimir Zhirinovsky in Russia's December 1993 parliamentary elections sent chills down the spines of many people all across the globe. After all, this is the same man who has threatened war with Germany, Japan, and even the United States.

Zhirinovsky's success becomes all the more foreboding when one considers just how quickly he has burst onto the Russian political landscape. A virtual *"who's he?"* in 1991 (many wish he would return there), Zhirinovsky is now riding atop the *"who's who"* on the world's scene. In fact, it's been well said that if Russian politicians were growth stocks, the best performer of 1991–1993 has been Vladimir Zhirinovsky.

Although immensely popular in his native Russia, Zhirinovsky is for all practical purposes a newcomer to the international scene. So much so, in fact, that much of his past still remains clouded in mystery. It almost seems like Zhirinovsky has just arisen from nowhere. Who is the real power behind this new political star? Are we to believe that Zhirinovsky himself is the only driving force behind the Liberal Democratic Party? Where does Zhirinovsky obtain his financial backing? Why has Zhirinovsky's rise to the top seemed so effortless—no snags, no hitches?

There are many, including some U.S. Intelligence sources, who believe that Zhirinovsky has strong ties with former members of the KGB (remember, the KGB was dismantled by Mikhail Gorbachev after the 1991 coup attempt). Insiders say that Comrade Zhirinovsky is being bankrolled by enemies of Boris Yeltsin, many of whom are former members of the KGB. Some even say that Zhirinovsky is a "rosebud" KGB captain who is intentionally creating political instability at the request of his bosses. As far as the KGB is concerned, Zhirinovsky expresses only admiration. According to an Associated Press article dated February 5, 1994, Zhirinovsky was quoted as saying: *"I always loved the army, the KGB, and the police, but they never accepted me because I wasn't a communist."* Zhirinovsky has on more than one occasion vowed to resurrect the KGB after he comes to power.

Despite Zhirinovsky's denials, the rumors continue to circulate about his KGB connection. As we have already seen, in the 1980s Zhirinovsky worked for an organization called the Soviet Peace Committee, which was nothing more than a KGB-sponsored Soviet propaganda house. It was also during this time that Zhirinovsky was active in *Shalom*, a state-sponsored Jewish group. Although outwardly pro-Jewish, *Shalom* was organized by the Anti-Zionist League, which was a KGB front organization. It was the purpose of *Shalom* and the Anti-Zionist League to create divisions among Soviet Jews.

Zhirinovsky's past is filled with mysterious connections that have seemingly cleared the way for his rise to power. As we have already seen, Zhirinovsky spent his early years at Moscow State University's Institute of Oriental Languages, which many feel was a KGB-affiliated section of the university. It was here, experts say, that the KGB trained some of its most gifted agents in foreign languages and cultures. In fact, Yevgeny Primakov, who now heads the Russian foreign intelligence service (the revamped KGB) has for years been the top man at the Institute of Oriental Languages. Therefore, it is possible that this is where Zhirinovsky was initially discovered and recruited. Zhirinovsky would have been an attractive prospect given his talent for learning foreign languages. Zhirinovsky is fluent in English, French, German, and Turkish, as well as his native Russian.

The most compelling evidence linking Zhirinovsky to the KGB, however, surrounds the 1989 formation of his Liberal Democratic Party. According to a February 1994 article by Jack Anderson and Michael Binstein, Zhirinovsky once again seemed to have friends in high places.

> *"Vladimir Zhirinovsky's Liberal Democratic Party was the first opposition party allowed in the then-Soviet Union. Intelligence reports claim that the KGB was busily looking for agents to form political parties once it became clear that President Gorbachev was going to allow multiple parties. Zhirinovsky's Liberal Democratic Party became the first non-communist party ever to register with the Soviet Justice Ministry, even though Zhirinovsky had few supporters at the time and didn't have the requisite five thousand signatures that the law required."*

Once again, Zhirinovsky is quick to dispel accusations that he was—and possibly still is—a KGB asset. Zhirinovsky recently told reporters:

"I would have been happy if the KGB helped me. If they would have, I would not be sitting here with you right now. I would be sitting in the Kremlin."

CONCLUSION

Is Vladimir Zhirinovsky a KGB operative? Experts are still divided. Regardless of his KGB connections, Zhirinovsky is one **Ka**G**e**y **B**ear that needs to be watched very closely over the coming months. Let's now take a look at some other significant factors that have helped propel Vladimir Zhirinovsky into political prominence in Russia.

Chapter Three

UNBEARABLE
CONDITIONS

BREAKING UP IS HARD TO DO

The break-up of the Soviet Union and the subsequent advent of shock-therapy economic reforms have literally created mass chaos in Russia today. Hyperinflation, exploding crime rates, diseases, plagues, food shortages, and environmental disasters are ravaging the lives of untold millions of Russians.

As the situation in Russia continues to worsen, ultranationalist Vladimir Zhirinovsky continues to gain momentum . . . momentum that if left unchecked could propel him into the Russian presidency by 1996 or sooner. Zhirinovsky has promised that when he is elected, Russia will once again begin to flex her military muscle in an effort to revive the great Russian Empire.

With conditions like these, there can be no doubt that Russia is a more dangerous threat today than she ever has been before. Like a wounded mother bear who has been robbed of her cubs, Russia is poised to become violently aggressive once again. In his January 12, 1992 article entitled "Slouching Into Chaos," Robert Cullen, writing for the *Los Angeles Times* agrees:

> *"If the people of Russia become poorer and more desperate, they will become like a cornered bear. When a bear is cornered, she rears up on her hind*

*legs and lashes out. All the Russian people need is an
ideology and a leader to direct their anger."*

With the advent of Vladimir Zhirinovsky, it would appear that the Russian people now have just such a leader. A
leader whose geopolitical vision is for Russia to realize her
destiny and make her "final dash to the south." Let's take a
closer look at the severity of present conditions in Russia that
make it ripe for the rise of a man like Vladimir Zhirinovsky.

ONLY THE GOOD DIE YOUNG

If you are like me, when you think about what it must be
like to live in Russia the images that come to mind are those
of stark economic poverty, extremely cold winters, nasty living conditions, and brutish violence. Well, just when you
thought living in Russia couldn't get any worse—it has! According to the Committee on Statistics (a Russian govern-
mental agency) the average life expectancy of Russian men
plummeted last year from sixty-two years of age to fifty-nine
years of age. That is a three year drop in one year! So, not
only is life in Russia miserable, it is getting shorter as well.
To put this in perspective, men in the United States can expect to live to the age of seventy-two and a half (that's thir-
teen and a half years longer than the average Russian male),
and America's figures are not dropping; they are improving.

*"It's just an incredibly clear picture of a society in cri-
sis,"* says David Coleman, university lecturer in demograph-
ics at Oxford University, who has focused on population trends
in Eastern Europe and the former countries of the Soviet
Union. Coleman goes on to say:

> *"A decline in life expectancy this dramatic has
> never happened in the post-war world. It is very stag-
> gering. It shows the malaise of society, the lack of*

public health awareness, and the fatigue associated with people who have had to fight a pitched battle their whole lives just to survive" (*New York Times*, 3/6/94).

"It is a spectacular decline, the largest one-year decline since the war," says Murray Feshbach, research professor of demography at Georgetown University in Washington, D.C. *"This drop is really unprecedented for any developed country. Russia's life expectancy figures are now below all major industrialized countries"* (AP, 2/6/94).

According to Feshbach, Russia's standard of living and life-span projections are rapidly approaching those of underdeveloped third world nations. In other words, men in Indonesia, the Philippines, and parts of Africa live longer than the average man in Russia.

Yevgeny B. Mikhailov, vice-president of Russia's State Committee on Statistics has this to say about the life expectancy figures: *"This is bad even by the standards of the Third World. To find statistics worse than these, one would have to look to very poor countries like Pakistan and Bangladesh"* (*New York Times*, 3/6/94).

Think about it! The mighty Russian bear, the superpower that once was the Soviet Union, is now literally in a free-fall as far as quality and quantity of human life are concerned.

But wait a minute, that's not all! Russian men are not the only ones who are experiencing this reduced life expectancy. Russian women are also living shorter lives as well. According to the State Committee on Statistics, life expectancy for Russian women declined from 73.8 years of age in 1992 to 73.2 years of age in 1993. This is equivalent to an eight-month drop in the average age of Russian women in just one year. Although these figures are not nearly as serious as those for Russian men—try telling that to Russian women. I can assure you, they are most troubled.

According to Murray Feshbach, these startling drops in the life expectancy tables for residents of Russia are by no means a one-year statistical anomaly. No! In fact, these figures just simply quantify the latest and most dramatic drop in what can only be described as a downward death spiral for the Russian populace. Feshbach's statistics clearly show that this downward trend began between the years 1988 and 1989. In fact, as recently as 1988-89, men in Russia could expect to live until the ripe old age of sixty-seven and Russian women even longer—seventy-four years of age. But today, just six years later, Russian men are only living to age fifty-nine and Russian women to age seventy-three. Thomas Hobbes, the seventeenth century English philosopher, was right when he said, *"Life without a powerful king is poor, nasty, brutish, and short."* Is it any wonder that so many Russians desperately long for someone—anyone—to come in and improve their quality and quantity of life.

R.I.D.S.
(RUSSIAN INFANT DEATH SYNDROME)

The infant mortality rate in Russia is also worsening. Infant mortality rose from 17.8 deaths per one thousand children in calendar year 1992 to 19.3 deaths per thousand children in calendar year 1993.

In a related statistic, the number of children born to the average Russian woman is also showing a rapid decline. In 1989, the average Russian woman could be expected to give birth to 2.17 children over the course of her lifetime. Today, that figure has fallen to slightly more than 1.4. In other words, fewer children are being born to Russian families and of the ones that are born, fewer of them are surviving past their first birthday.

These decreasing birth rates are not surprising to demographic experts. Experts say that in times of economic chaos and political upheaval, families choose to have fewer and fewer children. In fact, demographers say that this is a trend that is prevalent all across Eastern Europe today. But nowhere are the numbers more startling than in Russia.

These disturbing statistics remind me of what the Lord Jesus said in Matthew 24:19–21 as he warned those who would enter that future period of judgment referred to as the Great Tribulation. Jesus said:

> *"And woe unto them that are with child, and to them that give suck in those days! . . . For then shall be great tribulation, such as was not since the beginning of the world to this time, no, nor ever shall be."*

With conditions this harsh, it almost seems as if the nation of Russia has entered its own a mini-Tribulation period, as life itself has become more and more unbearable.

HONEY, I SHRUNK THE POPULATION!

If plummeting life expectancy rates, rising infant mortality rates and rapidly decreasing birth rates were not bad enough, Russia is also experiencing a death wave of unprecedented proportions. Russia's overall death rate is skyrocketing! The combination of all these negative factors has ignited a virtual population implosion in Russia today.

In 1991, Russia's overall death count exceeded its live birth count by two hundred and seven thousand. In 1993, deaths exceeded births by a grisly eight hundred thousand. Figures like these make Russia the first industrialized country in history to experience such a sharp overall decrease in population for reasons other than war, famine, or plague. If this trend continues unchecked (and experts say it is intensifying), then Russia's population of one hundred and fifty million will shrink drastically in the coming years.

The graph below shows that Russia has become a country that is so confused and uncertain about its future that it has all but stopped producing children, while at the same time its existing population is dying off at record pace.

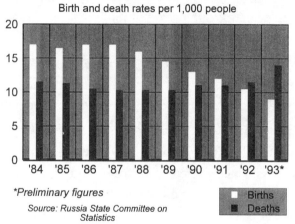

Russia's Population Implosion
Birth and death rates per 1,000 people

*Preliminary figures

Source: Russia State Committee on Statistics

TRAUMA CENTER

Yet another indicator of just how harsh conditions are in Russia is the number of traumatic deaths recorded. In today's Russia, death by trauma seems to be the death of choice. The number of Russians who die each year because of a traumatic event is rapidly rising. Trauma deaths include suicides (which account for over one-third of all unnatural deaths in Russia), murders, military casualties, on-the-job accidents, and poisonings.

Trauma death became the third leading cause of death in Russia in 1993. It had been the fifth leading cause of death in 1992. *"This is the saddest of facts in Russia today—the fact that so many people are dying in ways that are unnecessary. It is very depressing,"* says Aleksander I. Tkachenko, chief of the Russian Labor Ministry's Human Resource Department (*New York Times,* 3/6/94).

WHAT'S UP DOC?

Doctor Vladimir Z. Kucherenko, head of the Department of Social Medicine at Moscow's Sechenov Medical Academy, sums up the dire condition of the Russian people as follows: *"These figures quantify for us very clearly what the Russian people are feeling in their bones: poverty, violence, disease, and stress are taking a huge toll on public health"* (AP, 2/6/94).

What in the world could be causing life expectancy in Russia to be dropping so rapidly? *"It's a multifaceted problem,"* says Dr. Kucherenko. He continues:

> *"There are many reasons for this problem, and it is very hard to apportion a particular share of the blame to each contributor. But suffice it to say these are very difficult times for the Russian people and people are just not living as long. Our current overall socioeconomic difficulties certainly play a major part in this problem."*

In a recent article entitled "Rebuilding Russia," Russian exile and Nobel prize winning author Alexander Solzhenitsyn gives us the big picture of why living conditions are so bad in Russia:

> *"We have saddled our people with backbreaking, impossibly burdensome labor, torn them from their children, and have abandoned the children themselves to disease, brutishness, and the mere semblance of education. Our health care is utterly neglected, there are no medicines, and we have even forgotten the*

meaning of a proper diet. Millions lack housing and a helplessness bred of the absence of personal rights permeates the entire country" (*New Perspectives Quarterly*, Fall 1991).

Based on the avalanche of troubling statistics and expert analysis, it would seem that life in Russia is becoming more unBEARable in every way imaginable. Let's take a look at some of the major contributors to Russia's rapidly declining public health.

The four major factors are: diet, pollution, economic upheaval, and crime.

YOU ARE WHAT YOU EAT

The first factor that has contributed to a shorter lifespan for Russians is their diet. Although starvation is still uncommon, the real problem lies in the overall worsening of the average Russian diet. The price of meat, poultry, and fresh fruits and vegetables is skyrocketing and wages are unable to keep pace. The average Russian may be freer, but now he cannot afford to eat.

In the next chapter we will examine the negative impact that pollution has had on the Russian population.

Chapter Four

GODZILLA AND THE SMOG MONSTER

A second contributing factor to Russia's declining public health is pollution. The environmental consequences of seventy years of communist industrial policies have had dire effects on the health of millions of Russians. In his book entitled *Ecocide in the USSR—Health and Nature Under Siege*, Murray Feshbach writes:

> *"When historians finally conduct an autopsy on the Soviet Union and Soviet Communism, they may reach the verdict of death by ecocide. . . . It would be a unique but not an implausible conclusion. No other great industrial civilization so systematically and so long poisoned its land, air, water, and people. None so loudly proclaiming its efforts to improve public health and protect nature so degraded both. . . . In land area, the Soviet Union was the largest country in the world. Yet it beggard itself by endangering the health of its population—especially its children and its labor force—the productivity of its soil and the purity of its air and water."*

In his book, Feshbach describes how Russian factories in the Ural Mountains spew out smog, blanketing entire cities in soot. In some farming districts, the use of pesticides is so intensive that cancer has become the only cause of death. Also, an estimated three-fourths of the nation's surface water is polluted. According to Feshbach, untreated waterborne agricultural, industrial, and human wastes together threaten to kill the Sea of Azov, the Black Sea, and the Caspian Sea, and have turned giant rivers including the Volga, the Dniepr, and the Don into open sewers. The Volga, source of drinking water for thousands of Russian towns, is reported to be full of caustic chemicals.

"There is no worse ecological situation on the planet than ours in the USSR," says Dr. Grigory Matveyevich Barenboim, a leading Russian environmental analyst. He continues:

> *"It was said one hundred and fifty years ago that it was Russia's fate to serve as an example to the world of how not to live. I would say that we have become both an environmental testing ground for the whole world and an ecological threat to the entire planet."*

Russia has indeed proven to be an ecological threat not only to themselves but also to the whole world. Let's look at two of Russia's most infamous environmental disasters.

CHINA SYNDROME

In the early hours of April 26, 1986, a series of operator errors unleashed a power surge that literally blew the roof off reactor number four at Russia's Chernobyl nuclear power station. The blast, which triggered a partial meltdown of the core's fuel, was the worst reported accident in the history of the harnessed atom. The Chernobyl explosion poured more radioactive material into the atmosphere than had been released in the atomic bombings of Hiroshima and Nagasaki. The Soviet Union did not publicly acknowledge the disaster until April 28, two days after it happened. It seems that the obsession for concealing ugly realities, regardless of how potentially threatening they might be to others, is an ingrained

Russian trait. Over a period of ten days, a mile-high pillar of radioactive gas and particles traveled northwest from Chernobyl, then south and east, depositing radioactive contaminants from Scandinavia to Greece. The cleanup costs associated with the Chernobyl explosion continue to climb even today. The current estimate is roughly nine billion rubles and counting. Total economic losses could reach as high as two hundred billion rubles. To this day, Chernobyl ranks as the single worst ecological disaster in mankind's history.

THE DEAD SEA

On par with the Chernobyl nuclear catastrophe of 1986 is the killing of the massive Aral Sea. The Aral Sea, once larger than any of the Great Lakes (with the exception of Superior), is disappearing from the face of the earth. The Aral still remains Central Asia's second largest body of land-locked water, after the Caspian Sea, despite the fact that it has lost over forty percent of its surface area since 1960. The once-mighty Aral has had so much of its source water diverted for agriculture that little remains to feed the lake and counteract the evaporation process. The Aral has in essence become a new Dead Sea, surrounded by huge salt marshes and flats. The waters of the Aral dry to salt and blow away as noxious dust to strike the surrounding populace with illness and death. The sea is an ongoing environmental tragedy. If conditions are not improved, the Aral will continue to shrink in size. Experts estimate that by the year 2000 the Aral will have shrunk to two-thirds of its present size. Murray Feshbach writes:

> *"On the Aral's southern shores, just north of Turkmenistan, the earth no longer smells like soil but like chemicals. The local waters are full of chemical*

residues which have been washed back from irrigated lands. The level of chemicals is so high that the fish die. Data from the area indicates that two out of every three people examined in public health dispensaries are ill—mainly with typhoid, cancer of the esophagus, and hepatitis. . . . Worst of all, most of the sick are children. In many cases, doctors are recommending against breast-feeding because mothers' milk is thought to be toxic. . . ."

Like the rest of Russia, the once beautiful Aral Sea has been changed into a disaster zone, unfit for human existence.

THE SMOG MONSTER

Russia's most dangerous environmental threat may come in the form of Vladimir Volfovich Zhirinovsky. If Zhirinovsky comes to power he could very well hurl Russia straight toward ecocide. Zhirinovsky seems all too eager to get his hands on Russia's arsenal of nuclear weapons and stockpiles of radioactive waste. Listen to Zhirinovsky's cavalier attitude toward the nuclear bomb and its radioactive by-products:

"I will not hesitate to deploy atomic weapons to stop Germany and Japan from meddling in Russian affairs."

"I will not hesitate to practice nuclear blackmail against the West in order to feed the hungry Russian masses."

"I'll bury radioactive waste along the Lithuanian border and put up powerful fans and blow the stuff across at night. They'll all get radiation sickness. They'll die of it. When they either die out or get down on their knees, I'll stop."

"If Japan should press its demands for the Kurile Islands, I will sail our large navy around their small little island and if they so much as chirp I will nuke them."

"The West will pay Russia not to use its nuclear weapons against Europe."

With talk like this, Russia's worst environmental nightmares may yet still be in the future—the very near future if Vladimir Zhirinovsky assumes power.

The following poem by Russian Nikolai Kluyev, written in 1934, seems almost prophetic when one considers Russia's present ecological landscape.

The news we received was bitter
the rippling waves of the Aral sea in dead ooze,
the storks rare in the Ukraine,
the feather grass drooping in Mazdok,
and in the bright Sarov desert
the wheels of machines squealing underground.
Black clouds brought us further news;
the blue Volga is getting shallow,
evil men in Kerzhents are burning
the green pine fortresses,
the Suzdal wheat fields bring forth
lichen and stubble.
The cranes call to us
as they are forced to fly in for remains.
The nesting finches' feathers fall out
and they're plagued by ravening aphids,
the furry bees have only
the big veteran mushrooms to buzz at.
The news was black:
that there was no home land left . . .

Chapter Five

BEAR MARKET

In January of 1992 Russian President Boris Yeltsin freed prices for the first time in more than seven decades. Thus, the Russian government began one of the most daring economic reforms ever undertaken in the history of the world—the transformation of a centralized communist economy into a free-market economy. Needless to say, this is an experiment on an unprecedented scale. The country of Russia had been set on a crash course (no pun intended) toward a free-market economy.

The freeing of prices has been only part of the shock-therapy program that the government has initiated. The Russian government is simultaneously introducing a massive privatization of industry initiative, as well as agricultural reforms that will break up state-run collective farms. The new reform-minded government is also introducing tough new monetary and fiscal policies as well. One economist was quoted as saying: *"All this is like jumping out of an airplane while you are still sewing the parachute. But Russia has no choice—its plane is crashing."*

Needless to say, Russia's economy is in a state of confusion. Let's take a close look at Russia's leading economic indicators.

INFLATION

Inflation in Russia is currently running at twenty-five percent per month! Experts fear that inflation may rise as high as fifty percent per month by summer's end (1994). Inflation rates like these eat up wage increases, demoralize Russian workers, and turn the life savings of many Russian people into worthless paper. Experts believe that Russia is teetering on the brink of hyperinflation. In Ukraine, the inflation rate is currently one hundred and fifty percent per month.

INDUSTRIAL OUTPUT

Industrial output is an indicator of a nation's productivity or lack thereof. Russia's industrial output fell twenty-five percent in 1993, the sharpest one-year decline ever recorded. Experts are forecasting another twenty percent drop in 1994.

CONSUMER SPENDING

Consumer spending is simply an indicator of consumer confidence in the economy. In Russia, consumer spending plummeted thirty-eight percent in 1992 alone. To put this in perspective, during the entire period of our own country's depression (1929-33) consumer spending fell only twenty-one percent. Also, it is important to keep in mind that the standard of living in Russia in 1990 was worse than that of America in 1929.

UNEMPLOYMENT

Unemployment in Russia is so bad that figures are not even being published. Add to this the fact that the wages of as many as twenty million Russians are currently in arrears.

DEVALUATION OF THE RUSSIAN RUBLE

The value of the Russian ruble has declined some fifteen

percent against the dollar in the last twelve months alone. In 1992, the official exchange rate was one American dollar equals five hundred Russian rubles. Today the exchange rate is one American dollar equals twenty-five hundred Russian rubles (even more on the black market). Experts project that by the end of 1994 the exchange rate will be one American dollar equals ten thousand Russian rubles.

RUSSIA'S ECONOMIC FORECAST: HYPERINFLATION

The previously mentioned indicators show us very clearly that Russia's economy is on the verge of total collapse. To make matters even worse, on January 26, 1994 Boris Yeltsin's top economic aide, pro-reformer Boris Fyodorov, quit his position as Russia's finance minister saying:

> *"The Russian government has become nothing but a group of red managers who will do nothing but provoke economic collapse and social unrest by reviving a Soviet-style economy. . . . The threat of an economic and social explosion is now very much a reality"* (*Time*, 1/31/94).

In his farewell announcement at the Kremlin, Fyodorov went on to predict that Russia will soon be faced with soaring inflation (fifty percent per month by end of 1994), a dollar exchange rate of ten thousand rubles, devaluation of savings, unparalleled shortages, mounting capital flight, and isolation from world markets as old guard communist economic managers regained control of the fragile Russian economy. Jeffery Sachs, a professor of international trade at Harvard and economic advisor to the Russian government, agrees with Fyodorov. Sachs, writing in the January 31, 1994 issue of *The New Republic,* says:

"The new government is going to pursue danger-ous policies. The communist old guard has retaken all the power positions. Russia has been living on the verge of hyperinflation for two years. Inflation could get completely out of control and create profound social and political instability."

According to Sachs, hyperinflation is always the result of inept government fiscal policy.

"Hyperinflation is the result of government prac-tices. But the people who have been fighting to stop the rampant printing of money are gone. The people who are now in power have very little self-control. The restraints to inflation that existed are now gone. In the Ukraine, where there has been a reform-com-munist government like the one that currently exists in Russia the inflation rate is one hundred and fifty percent a month—second highest in the world."

Western observers have long insisted that the most dan-gerous threat to Russia's fragile economy is hyperinflation. It is feared that the current powers controlling Russia's economy do not fully understand how to keep inflation from spinning out of control.

MAGOG MISERY INDEX

In their January/February 1993 edition, the *Bulletin of Atomic Scientists* printed the results of a recent poll taken in Russia's capital city of Moscow. The poll was conducted by Moscow's MNENIE (Opinion) Service. The poll, which was taken by telephone, sheds much light on how Muscovites feel about the economic changes in their country.

Question #1—"For you personally, and your family have

the current reforms and price increases been catastrophic, or are you coping with it?"

	Apr. '91	Feb. '92	Mar. '92
Catastrophic	59	55	56
Coping	28	41	40
Don't Know	14	4	4

Question #2—"Are you and your family facing actual hunger because of the reforms?"

	Apr. '91	Feb. '92	Mar. '92
Yes	28	28	40
No	55	60	51
Don't Know	17	12	9

It is apparent from this data that the majority of Russians see their current economic situation as catastrophic. In fact, the data shows that many Russians are actually experiencing hunger as a result of the economic distress. One recent poll showed that only one out of five Russians say they are better off today than they were under communism (*U.S. News and World Report*, 3/7/94).

A TALE OF TWO POCKETBOOKS

Russia's recent move toward a free market economy has created the best of times and the worst of times for its people. On the one hand, the Russian people now enjoy freedoms that they never dreamed possible. Many Russians have seized the moment and are thriving under the new economic policies. In Russia, where about eighty percent of the population lives at or below the poverty level, fortunes are springing up practically overnight. This new breed of Russian entrepreneur is adapting well—profiting handsomely from the collapse of communism. As expected, free market reforms have given birth to a whole new class of wealthy Russian capitalists. An unimaginably rich social class is emerging. Russia has become a country of conspicuous haves and virtually ignored have-nots.

WHEELS OF FORTUNE

In the February 1994 edition of *World Press Review*, Slawomir Popowski writes the following account about one millionaire in Magog.

> *"On July 15, 1993 the first Rolls-Royce showroom in Eastern Europe opened on Mytna Street in Moscow, not far from the Lenin statue where communist demonstrations used to be held. Within three hours, the first client arrived and picked out the most expensive car on display—the $262,000 Silver Spur II. The happy buyer was a "businessman" from Yekaterinburg (formerly Sverdlovsk) whose name was not revealed. He had arrived in Moscow on a privately chartered plane, which he then used to ship his limousine beyond the Ural Mountains. He brought the money for the car in a suitcase."*

MANSIONS IN MAGOG

During my research on Russia's new capitalists I came across an article in the February 1994 edition of *The European*, written by Peter Conrad and Alejandra Sarmiento, entitled "High-Tech Castles of Kitsch." In this article the authors describe how these days, some wealthy residents of Moscow are able to live in style and they rather enjoy it.

> *"The dreary old Soviet-style interiors with flowery wallpaper and dark heavy sideboards are out.*

Modern Italian and Scandinavian design are what's in. With disposable incomes that would make their Eastern European neighbors envious, the Muscovite nouveau riche are indulging as never before on home renovations. Old kitchens, bathrooms, bedrooms, and living rooms are being torn out and replaced with the best money can buy. There are an estimated forty renovation and interior design companies already in business in Moscow. . . . Those who might wish to escape the confines of the city are in increasing numbers moving to dachas in the unspoiled Russian countryside. These dachas are typically big buildings, many of which have Russian baths, billiard rooms, and swimming pools."

MISERY IN MAGOG

As we have seen, there are those in Russia who are prospering as a result of the new economic reforms. On the other hand, these same policies of economic reform have devastated many millions of other Russians. As a result of the reformist policies, large numbers of Russian workers have lost their jobs or have simply been displaced as privatization of industry continues at break-neck pace. Russia's great economic experiment has fostered a brutish capitalistic feeding frenzy. In a recent editorial entitled "The Struggle for Russia's Soul," Mortimer Zuckerman wrote:

"This cowboy capitalism is manifesting itself in the emergence of a lavish lifestyle among a flamboyant and vulgar new middle class of businessman. This new middle class is made up mostly of speculators, traders, and outright criminals, all of whom are stealing the country blind. Now there is a contempt for

capitalism more intense than even the communists were able to engender with their years of Western propaganda" (U.S. News and World Report, 3/7/94).

Now certainly all of the blame for Russia's current economic instability cannot be laid at the feet of Boris Yeltsin and the reformers. It is common knowledge that the old Soviet Union had been in economic decline for years. In fact, long before Mikhail Gorbachev took control, the Soviet economy had been sputtering. During Gorbachev's six years of power the Soviet economy was characterized as being in steep decline. As recently as 1991 (some two years before the arrival of the reformers) the doomsday prophets were saying that the empire was bankrupt and that Soviet cities would soon be experiencing starvation conditions if drastic measures were not taken. It was at this time that oil production had fallen sharply. The Soviet budget deficit had reached a new high of twenty percent GNP. Most all Soviet foreign debt was in default. Farmers were hoarding grain. Inflation was accelerating. All of this was present long before Russia's economic reformers came on the scene.

The bottom line is that Russia's economy has been in significant decline for the last decade. It appears that even the current shock therapy switch to a free-market economy may prove to be a case of "too little too late" for the salvation of the Russian economy.

CONCLUSION

Russia's populace, disoriented by the sweeping changes and buckling under increased economic hardships, is rapidly running out of its much talked about patience. President Yeltsin's chances of successfully accomplishing economic reforms have all but evaporated with the resignation of reformist deputy prime minister Yegor Gaidar and pro-market finance minister Boris Fyodorov. As the pain associated with lower standards of living, unemployment, soaring inflation, and shortages becomes more intolerable, Russians are turning in greater and greater numbers to Vladimir Zhirinovsky. The threat of a general economic and social collapse is very likely to tilt Russian politics in favor of nationalistic extremism, thus handing the country over to someone like Zhirinovsky in the 1996 presidential election (if not sooner).

Chapter Six

COMRADES IN CRIME

Since the fall of communism in 1991, organized crime activity in Russia has mushroomed. Both insiders and outsiders alike will agree that organized crime gangs are literally taking over the country. One top-level Russian government report has laid out the extent of organized crime's predominance in the following stark terms: *"Organized crime has Russia by the throat! It is squeezing the life out of the private sector and holding the government itself hostage!"*

Conditions are so bad that Russia today is being compared to gangland Chicago or New York during the 1920s and '30s. You remember those days, don't you? Those were the days of Al Capone, Baby Face Nelson, and Machine Gun Kelly. Those were the days in America's history when mobsters, hoods, and thugs built and controlled vast criminal empires. The building blocks of these crime syndicates were the unlawful practices of racketeering, extortion, prostitution, bootlegging, kidnapping, and gambling. Believe it or not, this is Russia today! Mortimer Zuckerman, editor-in-chief of *Newsweek* magazine, has said, *"Day-to-day life in Moscow and other major cities is dominated by Mafia-type criminal gangs who make Al Capone look like a Boy Scout"* (*Newsweek*, 3/7/94).

Stephen Handelman, a visiting scholar at Columbia University and ex-Moscow bureau chief for the *Toronto Star* has said this concerning the growth of Russia's organized crime groups: *"It is safe to say that organized crime is the most explosive force to emerge from the wreckage of Soviet Communism" (Foreign Affairs,* March/April 1994).

According to Handelman, the emergence of the so-called Russian mafia has had three major effects on the country as a whole. Organized criminal gangs have:

1. Undermined economic and political reform
2. Spawned extraordinary levels of violence in major cities
3. Helped fuel a growing ultranational backlash

In other words, Handelman, like many other Russian experts, realizes that Russia's new crime syndicate constitutes a serious threat to post-Soviet democracy.

IN CAHOOTS

Rampant crime is bad enough but an atmosphere of rampant crime mixed with public officials who are corrupt or indifferent is far worse still. It is no mystery why the Russian mafia is so successful. The mob is successful because it is being nurtured, protected, supported, and encouraged by government officials at every level. Official corruption has in effect attacked the central nervous system of Russia's political and civil authority.

During the month of January 1994 the Russian newspaper *Izvestia* ran a special five-page documentary exposing the collusion that currently exists between mobster gangs and local Russian law enforcement officials. For example:

In the city of Tver, local police officers were making it a practice to inform city gangs whenever a vehicle with valuable cargo passed by a certain checkpoint.

In the same city of Tver, those who wished to open a new store, restaurant, or other place of business were having to go to city hall for their permit and then make a second stop to check in with local gang officials for final permission.

It is a widely known fact that the heads of Russian organized crime mobs are gathering detailed dossiers on all top-level officials and politicians.

Outside the city of Kazan farmers are forced by racketeers to make payoffs in exchange for "protection."

In the city of St. Petersburg there is reported to be an army of some ten thousand thugs and hoodlums, of which five hundred or more are known to be career criminals.

In St. Petersburg the police reported that after the collision between a car and a van, that the occupants of the car jumped out, gunned down the van's ten passengers, picked up their bodies, and drove off—all on a city street in broad daylight. Newspapers said that the police suspected gang warfare.

It is obvious from these examples that in Russia, organized crime gangs and public officials have joined forces to become partners in crime. In 1992, Russian government investigators reported that half the country's criminal groups had ties to the government. No doubt today the figures are even higher. Next we will examine how this crime explosion is affecting Russia's business climate.

LET THE BUSINESSES BEWARE

Russia's new open-market economy offers vast frontiers of potential opportunities and profits for shrewd entrepreneurs from all over the world. However, businesses must take careful steps to make sure of what they are facing. The potential gold mine of opportunity in Russian markets may quickly turn into a deep dark shaft of extortion, bribery, and payoffs if the businessman is not careful. Many a new venture has found itself doing business with "Russian partners" who were in reality just fronts for organized crime gangs. Russian entrepreneurs who try to play by the rules soon discover it is impossible to survive in the face of official and criminal competition. In the United States the rule of thumb in the marketplace has always been *caveat emptor—"let the buyer beware"*—but in Russia, the slogan has been changed to "let the businesses beware."

Control Risks Group, a highly respected international security firm, has said this about the extent of organized crime in Russia and its effect on the business climate:

> *"About five thousand organized crime groups engaged in racketeering, extortion, and kidnapping have surfaced in the former Soviet Union. . . . Russia has simply become the most dangerous place in the world for businesses to operate"* (*New York Times*, 1/30/94).

Stephen Handelman of Columbia University says: *"The 'mafia,' Russian-style, is a hydra-headed phenomenon that feeds on the emerging market economy of Russia."*

One top-level government report prepared for Russian president Boris Yeltsin recently reported that:

> *"Seventy to eighty percent of all Russian private enterprises and commercial banks located in major cities are forced to pay tributes of ten to twenty percent to organized crime"* (*New York Times*, 1/30/94).

This same report detailed how organized crime has successfully penetrated Russian banks by blackmailing, threatening, and in at least a dozen cases, killing bankers in order to gain access to their books. Once access is gained, organized crime leaders can better determine which companies and individuals are ripe for exploitation.

In 1993 alone, some ninety-four entrepreneurs were murdered. It is estimated that currently Russian organized crime syndicates control about forty thousand private businesses as well as two thousand or more in the state sector. It is obvious from these statistics that few, if any, Russian entrepreneurs can expect to remain in business for long without being asked to pay money or provide shares in their businesses to representatives of organized crime.

According to Russia's Ministry of Internal Affairs, organized crime controlled as much as forty percent of the turnover in goods and services in Russia during calendar year 1993. From these statistics it is clear that Russia's economy is rapidly being criminalized and there seems to be no end in sight.

Christopher Cross, executive director of Control Risks Information Services says this:

> *"Legitimate business is being scared away by the gangster style of trading which is now present in Russia. The lack of normal business practice is encouraging criminal activity and colossal amounts of corruption."*

This is obviously not the type of business environment that will appeal to international lenders and investors. Local crime lords and their greedy government allies have moved in to fill the vacuum created by the absence of any real civil authority. With bribe-taking bureaucrats on the one side and extortionists and racketeers on the other, doing business in Russia is becoming an increasingly difficult proposition.

A GANG IS A GANG IS A GANG

Here in the United States, gangs and organized crime groups seem content for the most part to control more traditional criminal vices such as the drug market, the prostitution market, and the gambling market. But in Russia this is not the case. In Russia, organized crime groups control all types of activity. The tentacles of Russian graft and corruption seem to extend to every facet of society. Stephen Handelman says:

> *"In the absence of government regulation, criminal cartels know no traditional criminal boundaries. These Russian mafia syndicates have infiltrated everything: banks, real estate markets, stock exchanges, and even the rock music industry. Most unsettling of all perhaps is the involvement of organized crime in the market of stolen Red Army weapons."*

Pyotr S. Filippov, an economist and former parliamentary deputy who now heads Russia's Analytical Center for Social and Economic Policies has stated:

> *"Over the last six months (9/93-2/94) the organized crime activity has become much worse because it has met with no resistance. Official reports have documented the current crime wave but no government action has been taken. When no one seems to be in charge, it's easy for the mobsters to just move right in"* (*New York Times*, 1/30/94).

In Russia today, it is clear that no one is in charge. Therefore, the criminal element has had freedom to infiltrate whatever arena they desire.

EXPORTING EXTORTION

Today's Russia is literally brimming over with organized crime. In fact, organized crime is quickly becoming one of Russia's biggest export items. Jayson Carcione, reporting for Reuters, has said:

> *"Russian gangs have literally spread their ten-*

tacles around the world—even to the Brighton Beach area of Brooklyn (an area of New York City heavily populated by Russian immigrants) and also through much of Europe. Many of these Russian mobsters have adopted mafia-style tactics, often demanding protection money from vulnerable shop keepers and businesses."

According to Carcione and other experts, there are now an estimated one hundred and fifty or more of these Russian gangs operating internationally, many of which have formed alliances with the Italian mafia. In fact, crime chiefs from Moscow and the Baltic states are known to have held crime "summits" with their counterparts in the Italian mob.

TOURIST TRAP

If left unchecked, the current crime wave in Russia will no doubt have devastating effects on the multimillion-dollar tourist industry. Gangland killings, gun shootouts, kidnappings, and bombings have become a normal part of daily existence in dozens of Russian cities. It is reported that guns and bodyguards are now a common part of Moscow life. It is the norm to see them at the finer public venues such as the theatre, cinema, and ballet. Rising crime rates have turned what was once an ordered society into a land of fearful strangers. One recent survey showed that three out of four residents of Moscow stated that they were afraid to walk the streets at night. Another survey showed that forty-nine percent of Russians rated crime higher on their list of concerns than unemployment. One Russian embassy spokesman was recently quoted as saying:

"It's not at all safe anymore to travel from Moscow to St. Petersburg. The crime situation has dete-

*riorated in the past two years. Unfortunately foreign-
ers, including businesses are many times the main
targets."*

It is reported that in the first six months of 1993 alone
there were seven thousand reported crimes committed against
foreigners, most of which were extortion demands.

INEFFECTIVE GOVERNMENT INTERVENTION

Over the last several years, the Russian government has
made several attempts to curb the rising tide of organized
crime within its borders, but all such attempts have met with
miserable failure. In fact, government intervention has had
just the opposite effect. Government officials in Russia have
inadvertently created the perfect environment for organized
crime growth. Overtaxation, heavy government regulation,
dismantling the last vestiges of the old communist police state,
and the absence of a strong judicial system all combine to
make Russia an almost perfect spawning ground for criminal
gangs. According to Stephen Handelman:

> *"Russian policymakers committed a fundamental
> mistake: they tried to develop a free market before
> constructing a civil society in which such a market
> could safely operate."*

These ineffective government policies coupled with a
police force that is indifferent, corrupt, and poorly equipped
(some officers are forced to pursue criminals by bus and taxi)
have made Russia a nation where crime pays. It is no wonder
that the average law-abiding Russian citizen finds himself
being drawn more and more into the dark world of organized
crime, graft, and corruption.

CATCHING THE RUSSIAN CRIME WAVE

It has been said that the Russian organized crime gang is

the only Soviet institution that actually benefited from the collapse of the communist republic. In a 1993 speech, Russian president Boris Yeltsin said that *"criminal gang activity has reached such a scale and character that it threatens the very future of the Russian state."* A frustrated Yeltsin explained that organized crime was *"destroying the economy, destabilizing the political climate, and undermining public morale." "Crime,"* Yeltsin said, *"has become problem number one for the Russian people."*

Yeltsin was not exaggerating! In the first year after the fall of communism, the Russian public prosecutor reported 2.7 million crimes, an increase of thirty-three percent over the previous year (1991). The following table depicts in a statistical fashion the rising tide of the current Russian crime wave. Note in particular the violent nature of these crimes. The increase in violent crimes is usually the most visible sign of an underworld feeding frenzy. Rival gangs are doing whatever it takes to gain a foothold in the new Russian free-market system.

Type of Crime	# of Instances in 1993	% Change from 1992
• Crimes committed by organized groups	355,000	up 28 %
• Crimes causing serious bodily injury	66,000	up 24 %
• Premeditated murder	29,200	up 27 %
• Crimes committed with guns	22,100	up 250 %

CRIME CZAR

One of the main reasons Vladimir Zhirinovsky is so attractive to the average Russian is because the average Russian wants the criminal element in the country removed. There is no doubt that the strong support for Zhirinovsky comes as much from the populist backlash against crime as it does from the backlash against economic reforms. Whenever economic discontent is coupled with anger over official government corruption and criminal violence, it becomes a potent political force. Russians long for a strong hand to fight crime and restore law and order in the market places and in the streets. Zhirinovsky seems to be just what the doctor ordered. He is tough and autocratic, a proponent of simple solutions at a time of growing disorder and chaos. In preparation for the December parliamentary elections, Zhirinovsky ran a campaign based on a harsh law and order platform.

In one of his typical pre-election television appearances Zhirinovsky told voters:

> *"If I am elected we will set up courts on the spot to shoot the leaders of criminal bands. Let us return to Russia's civil-war era decrees ordering the shooting of criminals on sight."*

> *"I may have to shoot one hundred thousand people, but the three hundred million others will live peacefully."*

"I voted for him because he is a stern guy and he will bring order," says Alexander Trishin, a forty-three-year-old tea salesman in Moscow, *"Russia is used to an iron fist."*

In a February 1994 speech Zhirinovsky, in vintage fashion, called upon all of Russia's spies and secret police to "clench their teeth" until he comes to power and unleashes them on a worldwide search for Russia's looted wealth.

> *"Stay at your posts, guard and gather information, search for 'werewolves' within your ranks and be ready for action."*

This outrageous rhetoric is "classic" Zhirinovsky. Zhirinovsky himself seems to be fascinated by the idea of secret agents, spies, and conspiracy theories. Typically he is either the victim of these conspiracies or he is the manipulator of them himself.

> *"If my party wins I will root out those who have betrayed Russia's interests and illegally enriched themselves. Corrupt officials will be at the top of the list. We will have to return everything that has been stolen to the people, we will smash mafia clans, punish unpatriotic criminals. We will find them wherever they are, in whatever hole they try to huddle in."*

This "hang 'em high" tough talk endears Zhirinovsky to millions of Russian voters. In fact, it is believed that if President Yeltsin's regime does not begin to take aggressive steps to curb the rising tide of organized crime and corruption then Yeltsin will in essence be turning over millions of votes to Zhirinovsky's populist movement. No doubt even Russia's entrepreneurial class will begin to swing its support away from Yeltsin and his reformers over to the protectionist policies of Zhirinovsky's Liberal Democratic Party. Stephen Handelman summarizes the problem well:

> *"As Russians increasingly identify free-market democracy with organized crime and corruption, they will turn toward much less congenial forms of governing. Unchecked economic chaos and gang violence could well foster the rise of a hostile authoritarian power on the Eurasian continent, instead of the prosperous partner the West requires for a stable twenty-*

first century world."

Could it be that this hostile authoritarian personality has already arrived? Vladimir Zhirinovsky's authoritarian, anti-crime rhetoric has made him Russia's most popular candidate for Crime Czar.

Chapter Seven

MASTER OF THE MEDIA

There can be no doubt about the fact that a large part of Vladimir Zhirinovsky's recent success at the polls is due to his campaigning style. Outrageous? You bet. Inflammatory? Most definitely. Blunt? Like a hammer. Entertainment value? Five stars!

While his rivals wasted free television time on boring monologues about debt financing and the benefits of monetarism, Zhirinovsky proved himself to be a master of the media. Zhirinovsky hardly mentioned anything about an economic policy (quite possibly because no such policy exists). To voters, Zhirinovsky seemed to be the only national figure in the campaign who was capable of speaking with a plain, unbureaucratic, and emotional voice. In the February 14, 1994 edition of *The New Republic*, Michael McFaul, a research associate at the Center for International Security and Arms Control at Stanford University, says:

> *"Zhirinovsky's television ads, a forum that will become even more important in future campaigns, were brilliant. Separate commercials were broadcast to appeal to every interest group from women to soldiers. His campaign message was simple and clear. The other opposition parties failed miserably (especially Russia's Choice). Their ads were excruciatingly long treatises on macroeconomic stabilization. Rather than targeting their responses to voter concerns, they promised more hardships not less."*

Victoria Pope, reporting in the December 13, 1993 issue of *U.S. News and World Report,* writes:

> *"In homespun television commercials, Zhirinovsky appealed to millions of Russians who feel like outsiders in Yeltsin's Russia. He just talked the way Russians talk at the kitchen table. His message reflects popular opinion."*

In a December 27, 1993 article for *Time* magazine, Jill Smolowe writes:

> *"For every constituency, he designed a tailor-made message. The military received pledges of a resurrected and expanded Russian Empire. Fixed-income pensioners and students were promised a decent standard of living. Crime-weary citizens were assured that gang leaders would be executed. Meanwhile, foreigners were offered up as scapegoats, and Jews were blamed for provoking anti-Semitism."*

In one television commercial Zhirinovsky appears with a bottle of vodka in one hand and a condom in the other saying: *"This is all that Gorbachev has left us."* In another Zhirinovsky is shown holding roses and a box of expensive chocolates as he pronounces with a roguish grin,

> *"Under my policies living standards will rise, male mortality rates will plummet, and presto—a husband in every bed. Every Russian woman will have a man of her own. There will be no lonely women in my Russia."*

This is just the type of outlandish behavior that has enabled Zhirinovsky, in just four short years, to become the most formidable force in the Russian political arena.

In yet another *Vladimercial,* Zhirinovsky is shown twirling an expensive brassiere, stating that if he were voted into office he would provide cheap underwear for his constituents. Zhirinovsky's wild behavior has become so popular with the Russian people that one Russian newspaper columnist reported that tapes of Zhirinovsky's speeches were outselling those of professional comedians. To many Russian voters Zhirinovsky's outrageous remarks prove that he is something that the other politicians aren't—he is sincere.

These media antics at times make it difficult not to treat Zhirinovsky as a buffoonish clown—a maniacal politician more deserving of ridicule than fear. But do not be deceived! Underneath the clown's mask is a clever, complex, and keenly shrewd politician who knows how to use publicity with remarkable effectiveness. History shows all too clearly the allure of clowns who know how to harness the discontent of the masses.

Zhirinovsky's Liberal Democratic Party has been able to do just that, bolstering some twenty-five percent of the nearly sixty million votes cast in Russia's December 12, 1993 parliamentary election (fourteen million of Russia's one hundred and five million eligible voters). With these strong numbers come sixty-seven house seats in the lower house of Russia's new parliament. During the campaign, Zhirinovsky dipped heavily into his campaign war chest and spent some three hundred million rubles ($250,000) in order to ensure that he was on television more than any of the other candidates. It is reported that Zhirinovsky was on the air a total of two hundred and twenty minutes during the last week of the campaign.

Through his media blitz, Zhirinovsky was successful in attracting the votes of millions of disenfranchised Russians. With his mastery of the media, Vladimir Zhirinovsky may well be the most astute political grandstander the nation of Russia has ever seen.

Chapter Eight

DEMA<u>GOG</u>

After losing the Soviet Empire and the Cold War, millions of Russians long for renewed status in the world. Russia is a country with a severely bruised national pride. Therefore, Russia is a nation ripe for the advent of a demagogue like Vladimir Zhirinovsky. *Webster's Dictionary* defines the word "demagogue" as, *"a leader championing the cause of the common people; a leader who makes use of popular prejudices, false claims, and promises in order to gain power."* It would seem that the only item missing from *Webster's* entry would be a picture of Vladimir Zhirinovsky in the margin.

According to Maria Mendras, a Russian specialist with the National Foundation of Political Science in Paris, Zhirinovsky relies more on his "shock jock" demagoguery than on any coherent policy.

> *"Zhirinovsky has no formal programs and offers no concrete alternatives, he simply reflects the mood of the population today, which does not want to see the continued deterioration of normal Russian life. Zhirinovsky's appeal is to the Russian soul and to Russian nationalism"* (Time, 12/27/93).

In a December 14, 1993 appearance on the *MacNeil/ Lehrer Newshour*, former Secretary of State James Baker said: *"This man Zhirinovsky can be very scary. It seems to me that at least he's a demagogue and at worst he is a clear fascist."*

Appearing on the same *MacNeil/Lehrer* broadcast was

Sergei Gregoriev, deputy press secretary to former Soviet president Mikhail Gorbachev and now a visiting professor at Northeastern University. Gregoriev had this to say concerning the persona of Zhirinovsky:

> *"We don't know much at all about Zhirinovsky's economic package because most of what he says is pure demagoguery, and we don't know much about his domestic policy either."*

In the December 15, 1993 edition of the *Wall Street Journal*, Elisabeth Rubinfien writes:

> *"Zhirinovsky's potent blend of national pride, xenophobia, paranoia, and authoritarianism appealed to the many people who feel that their country has been degraded and that reforms have brought only chaos."*

Alan Cooperman of the Associated Press says:

> *"Zhirinovsky's appeal to many Russians is clear. He deftly strikes a chord that has been drawn tight by Russia's national humiliation and suffering. After decades of Soviet propaganda, and centuries of czarist expansion, the loss of the empire hurts. So do economic disarray, rising crime, and the feeling of being prostrate before the United States."*

From these comments it appears clear that those who voted for Zhirinovsky seem to be more interested in a new, charismatic political face than the policies that lie behind it. One young Muscovite voter put it this way:

> *"Here is what I think: The leaders of other parties who have nominated their candidates are already in power. Zhirinovsky has not been in power. Let's*

give him a chance. Let's see what he will do."

Despite the lack of a brilliant new economic theory or a detailed social agenda, Zhirinovsky's popularity continues to rise. As best as I can tell, the "master of the world's political platform" consists of the following ten simple planks:

1. Immediately stop all aid from Russia to the former republics of the Soviet Union.
2. A reduction of personal as well as business taxes.
3. Bring Russia's military conversion to a grinding halt.
4. Increase the sale and export of Russian-made arms to help finance consumer imports.
5. Repudiate all debts run by the former Soviet Union, and terminate payments on Russia's foreign debt.
6. Liquidate the five thousand organized mafia gangs that have a strangle-hold on the country.
7. Form an alliance with Germany that would expand the borders of both nations at the expense of Central and Eastern European countries.
8. Unite all former Soviet republics into a new Russian federation.
9. Provide all military officers a homestead upon retirement.
10. Stop troop withdrawal from Eastern Europe, the Baltics, and other former Soviet Republics.

In Zhirinovsky's own words, *"these measures ought to double Russia's living standard in three to four months."*

WE CAN'T **BEAR** THE THOUGHT

To most people in the world, the very thought of a demagogue like Vladimir Zhirinovsky gaining power and thus being armed with nuclear weapons is too horrible to even contemplate. Therefore, most people try to dismiss him as too clownish, too hysterical, too bigoted ever to become a major factor in Russian politics. However, we must realize that Russia has entered a highly unstable transitional period where anything is possible. Zhirinovsky's uncanny ability to tap into the psyche of the Russian masses makes him a force to be reckoned with. In a December 27, 1993 *Newsweek* article, Carroll Bogert agrees:

> *"Zhirinovsky's slogans resonated like a cry from the nation's unconscious, articulating the repressed desires of a people weighed down by terrible suffering"*

Kevin Fedarko, writing for *Time* on December 27, 1993, echoes this same thought:

> *"Zhirinovsky has become immensely popular with the people by trawling the darker emotional currents of humiliation, impotence, and abandonment coursing through Russia's muddy provincial towns and overcrowded apartment blocks. His incessant hammering at the resentment generated by the country's plunge from great power to global beggar has made him a touchtone for the nation's deepest pathologies."*

Zhirinovsky's radical views and constant demagoguery have made him a most unwelcome visitor in more than one country. For example, Zhirinovsky was, for all practical purposes, thrown out of Bulgaria in December of 1993 after declaring that the country needed a new president. Zhirinovsky was later denied a visa by Germany. After being informed by a German diplomat that Germany had denied him an entry visa, Zhirinovsky replied, *"this action could very well lead to a new world war and Germany's destruction."* Meanwhile

France's European affairs minister, Alain Lamassoure, said that Zhirinovsky should think twice if he intends to visit Paris. *"If Mr. Zhirinovsky maintains his views, I don't see how we could welcome him in France."*

On yet another front, Zhirinovsky's unabashed intention to annex the three Baltic republics of Latvia, Estonia, and Lithuania into Russia have leaders of these countries scurrying to obtain international support for their continued independence. It is even reported that Estonia may actually give back the Russian-populated city of Narva, just so it can get rid of the six thousand Russian soldiers who are stationed there.

Eastern European countries are also suffering from a severe case of the jitters, especially when they hear Zhirinovsky make statements like:

"When I come to power Germany and Russia will divide up much of Eastern Europe."

After hearing these remarks, it is not surprising that Poland, the Czech republic, Slovakia, and Hungary have turned up the volume on their requests to be granted inclusion in NATO. It is also no wonder that Ukraine is clinging very tightly to its bank of nuclear weapons.

While the temptation is to dismiss most of Zhirinovsky's inflammatory discourse as merely the rhetoric of an ambitious demagogue, the volume and consistency of his threats is compelling evidence of his real thinking.

Chapter Nine

ZHIRINOVSKY BEAT

It goes without saying that Vladimir Zhirinovsky is already a household name for millions of Russians. Now, thanks to *Time* magazine, Zhirinovsky is fast becoming a household name in the United States as well. Beginning in January 1994 *Time* began running what they call "ZhirinovskyBeat" with each issue. Typically, these articles are partial-page pictorials chronicling "Mad Vlad's" latest escapades.

In *Time's* February 28, 1994 issue, "ZhirinovskyBeat" contains a collage of five exclusive photos of Russia's most popular ultranationalist. Photo #1—Zhirinovsky standing in front of his Moscow home; photo #2—Zhirinovsky playfully being pulled on a sled; photo #3—Zhirinovsky, clad only in his underwear, receiving a massage from a heavy-handed Russian masseur (a treat he gives himself several times a week); photo #4—Zhirinovsky in the shower spouting off to the photographer that he longs to one day swim naked in the Indian Ocean; photo #5—Zhirinovsky pulling a Jed Clampett-sized stack of rubles from a hidden safe in his home. The heading of the *Time* pictorial reads as follows:

> *"Whether he is at his office in Moscow or traveling abroad, Vladimir Zhirinovsky can't resist making bold statements about deadly new secret weapons or outlining his plans for the Russian annexation of Alaska. But after-hours he is just a regular guy."*

Make no mistake about it, Vladimir Zhirinovsky is no

ordinary Joe. *Time* magazine does not make it a habit of sending photographers half-way around the world to take Polaroids of "regular guys." Time, Inc. is in the business of selling magazines, and they understand that Zhirinovsky sells! *Time* magazine understands that Zhirinovsky may soon be more than just a loud-mouthed Russian ultranationalist—he may soon be the next president of Russia.

Chapter Ten

THE MAN WITH THE GOLDEN GUN

I guess I have seen just about all of the James Bond movies ever made. *Goldfinger, Diamonds Are Forever, Thunderball, From Russia With Love, The Spy Who Loved Me, Live and Let Die, Moonraker, Never Say Never*, the list seems to go on and on. Almost like a page out of an Ian Fleming spy novel comes Vladimir Zhirinovsky and his claim that he possesses a deadly new secret weapon known as the "Elipton." Quick, bring 007 out of retirement!

This is no joke! Zhirinovsky told reporters recently on a swing through Yugoslavia, *"this weapon has already killed twelve Muslim soldiers in Bosnia."* Zhirinovsky went on to say that he had given the go-ahead for the use of the "Elipton" weapon by Russian officers in the former Yugoslavia. According to Zhirinovsky:

> *"Some Russian officers in Serbia, thirty miles from Belgrade, in the front lines against Muslim military units used a little—one part—of the Elipton weapon against military units, and they had only twelve victims, only soldiers."*

Zhirinovsky maintains that the Elipton weapon kills by producing massive impulses of sound that humans are not able to withstand (sounds like Zhirinovsky is describing himself). The weapon reportedly leaves no visible marks or wounds—only nice clean corpses. Zhirinovsky explained the weapon to reporters in Serb-held Croatia as follows:

> *"There will not be a single trace of firearms wounds, not one drop of blood, not one damaged building."*

You might be surprised to know that in Ezekiel 38 and 39 the Bible does indeed speak of the use of secret weaponry. However, in the biblical account it is not Gog (Zhirinovsky) who will be wielding the ultimate weapon of mass destruction, but rather it is God. The Bible says that as the hordes of Gog storm down into the land of Israel, that the anger and blazing wrath of Almighty God will be ignited. Listen to Ezekiel 38:18–19:

> *"And it shall come to pass at the same time when Gog shall come against the land of Israel, saith the Lord GOD, that my fury shall come up in my face. For in my jealousy and in the fire of my wrath have I spoken, Surely in that day there shall be a great shaking in the land of Israel."*

Ezekiel goes on to record in 38:20–22 that it is at this time that God unleashes a heavenly flurry of destruction, the likes of which has not been seen since the days of Sodom and Gomorrah. A massive earthquake, pestilence, hailstones, confusion, fire, brimstone, and torrential rain will combine to thwart the evil plan of Gog. The Bible declares that on that day, Gog and his confederates will be totally decimated on the mountains of Israel.

Master of the Media: Vladimir Zhirinovsky may well be the most astute political grandstander the nation of Russia has ever seen.

Master of the Military: One of Zhirinovsky's most loyal constituents is the Russian military. "I see a proud Russia, a Russia wherein the glorious traditions of its army will once again be realized."

Master of the World: According to Zhirinovsky, the "Last Dash to the South" is Russia's destiny. "Russia will do what is foreordained and will fulfill its great historical mission. It is our fate."

The Master Blaster: Zhirinovsky has a penchant for the bombastic statement and an uncanny ability to both amuse and outrage in the same sentence.

The Imperial Ambitions of Vladimir Zhirinovsky

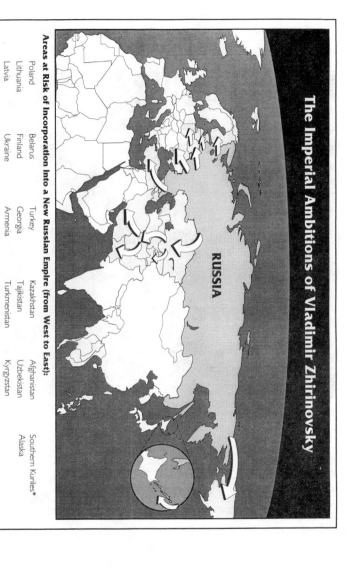

RUSSIA

Areas at Risk of Incorporation Into a New Russian Empire (from West to East):

Poland	Belarus	Turkey	Kazakhstan	Afghanistan
Lithuania	Finland	Georgia	Tajikistan	Uzbekistan	Southern Kuriles*
Latvia	Ukraine	Armenia	Turkmenistan	Kyrgyzstan	Alaska
Estonia	Moldova	Azerbaijan	Iran	Pakistan

*Occupied by Russia since 1945, the southernmost four islands of the Kurile chain are claimed by Japan.

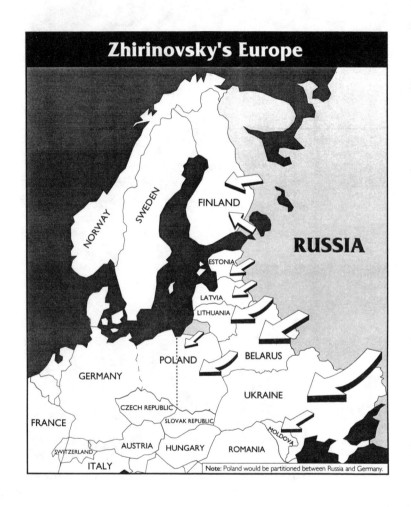

Zhirinovsky's Europe

NORWAY

SWEDEN

FINLAND

RUSSIA

ESTONIA

LATVIA

LITHUANIA

POLAND

BELARUS

GERMANY

UKRAINE

CZECH REPUBLIC

FRANCE

SLOVAK REPUBLIC

MOLDOVA

SWITZERLAND

AUSTRIA

HUNGARY

ROMANIA

ITALY

Note: Poland would be partitioned between Russia and Germany.

Владимир
ЖИРИНОВСКИЙ

ПОСЛЕДНИЙ
БРОСОК НА ЮГ

МОСКВА
1993

The Russian version of Zhirinovsky's autobiography *Last Dash to the South*. At this writing, no English version has been printed.

РОССИЯ – ОТЕЧЕСТВО ДЛЯ ВСЕХ.
ВСЕ НАРОДЫ – БОЛЬШИЕ И МАЛЫЕ –
РАВНЫ ПЕРЕД ЗАКОНОМ.
РУССКИЙ НАРОД ЯВЛЯЕТСЯ ГАРАНТОМ
БЛАГОПОЛУЧИЯ И ЦЕЛОСТНОСТИ
СТРАНЫ.

1993 № 8

Лидеру необходимы сила, здоровье, молодость,
честность и четкость

Zhirinovsky's *Falcon*—**a publication of Zhirinovsky's Liberal Democratic
Party**

Zhirinovsky's *Truth (Pravda)*—a publication of Zhirinovsky's Liberal Democratic Party

In Zhirinovsky's world, Russians are superior to other Slavs; China and Japan are not to be trusted; the United States is an aggressor nation destined to be punished in the future; and Russia's historic duty is to dominate and suppress the Muslim world—Turkey and Iran included.

Vladimir Zhirinovsky, leader of the Liberal Democratic Party and the most talented orator of Russia's far right.

ГОВОРЯТ, ВЛАДИМИР ЖИРИНОВСКИЙ
РАВНОДУШЕН К ЖЕНЩИНАМ...
ТАК ЛИ ЭТО?

КТО ОНА?

Узнавшего просим сообщить

в редакцию газеты

«Сокол Жириновского».

103045, Москва,

Рыбников пер., 1.

The photographs above, of Vladimir Zhirinovsky and an unidentified woman, appeared in issue no. 8 of *Zhirinovsky's Falcon*, a newspaper published by Russia's Liberal Democratic Party. The photos, which were published during the campaign, were part of an effort by Zhirinovsky to dispel rumors that he is gay. A headline over the photos read, THEY SAY VLADIMIR ZHIRINOVSKY IS INDIFFERENT TO WOMEN. OH, REALLY? Zhirinovsky is married and has a son.

Chapter Eleven

MAD ABOUT VLAD

As recently as one year ago, most of the world had never heard of Vladimir Volfovich Zhirinovsky. But over the last year, Zhirinovsky's name has literally been broadcast all around the globe. Zhirinovsky has been seen on television, in magazines, in newspapers, and in numerous government reports. Zhirinovsky's notorious behavior and bombastic rhetoric have attracted worldwide media attention. The entire world seems to be asking the question, *"Who is Vladimir Volfovich Zhirinovsky?"*

During my research for this book, I encountered all kinds of commentary concerning the person of Vladimir Zhirinovsky. Allow me to provide you with a brief catalog of these comments taken from Zhirinovsky watchers all around the world.

Sergei Grigoriantz, editor and political analyst for the Glasnost Information Agency (*The Jerusalem Post*, 1/29/94)

> *"The extreme nationalist alliance led by Vladimir Zhirinovsky will sooner or later take control of Russia, because there are no forces capable of counteracting it."*

> *"Zhirinovsky is worse than Stalin or Hitler because he has nuclear power."*

> *"The West does not understand the mentality of people like Zhirinovsky and does not take his territo-*

rial ambitions seriously."

"When Zhirinovsky gains power he will begin a war to gain territory, and there will be a threat to the entire civilized world."

Dr. Stuart Goldman, former professor of Russian history and presently an advisor with the Congressional Research Service in Washington, D.C.

"Zhirinovsky is power hungry and he will say and do anything that will attract an audience and secure votes."

"Zhirinovsky is a virulent racist who craves attention. His stock and trade is to attract attention to himself."

"Zhirinovsky wants to be president of Russia and he will be satisfied with nothing less."

Strobe Talbott, ambassador-at-large to Russia

"I am obviously concerned about the showing of the ultranationalist Liberal Democratic Party of Vladimir Zhirinovsky."

Bill Clinton, President of the United States

"I am concerned by some of the comments that have been made by Mr. Zhirinovsky, the leader of the so-called Liberal Democratic Party in Russia. I think no American, indeed no citizen of the world, who reads such comments could fail to be concerned" (*MacNeil/ Lehrer Newshour*, 12/15/93).

Oleg Kalugin, former KGB general

"The people of Russia are very angry and un-

stable. They are hungry for a strong leader. And some day if there is a leader who emerges, a prominent one, or authoritative enough to lead these people, they would follow him" (*MacNeil/Lehrer Newshour*, 1/13/93).

Anatoly Chubais, deputy prime minister of Russia (after the December 12, 1993 election results)

"Immediately we have to call Zhirinovsky's Liberal Democratic Party what it really is. It is neither liberal, nor is it democratic. It is the Fascist Party! We have to explain to the Russian people what a fascist is, and we have to explain what will happen if such a man is given the trust of the people."

James Baker, former Secretary of State under George Bush

"It isn't positive to see a man like Zhirinovsky, who espouses the views that he espouses achieve a significant percentage of the vote" (*MacNeil/Lehrer Newshour*, 12/14/93).

Andrei Olechowski, Polish foreign minister

"The news about Zhirinovsky's success is bad, simply bad. And of course, we in Poland are very worried. We are worried that a large segment of the Russian electorate seems to favor a totalitarian state and imperial foreign policy" (*MacNeil/Lehrer Newshour*, 12/15/93).

Sergei Kovalov, a leader in the pro-Yeltsin political party known as Russia's Choice

"The Russian people have been deceived by populist slogans, unrealized slogans, and cheap acting"

(*Wall Street Journal*, 12/15/93).

"With the advent of Vladimir Zhirinovsky, the threat of fascism in Russia has risen tall and high."

Ariel Cohen, Salvatori fellow in Russian and Eurasian studies at the Heritage Foundation in Washington, D.C. (Knight-Ridder/Tribune News Service, 12/27/93)

"Zhirinovsky means carnage for Russia and her neighbors."

"The bloody conflicts in Bosnia, Serbia, and Croatia will be dwarfed if the former Soviet Union erupts. History did not end in 1989. And it certainly did not become prettier."

"The success of Vladimir Zhirinovsky in the recent Russian elections has sent chills along the spines of many eastern Europeans and citizens of the former Soviet republics."

"It is tempting to dismiss Zhirinovsky's outrageous autobiography as a political polemic. But a failed Austrian painter and former army corporal was similarly ignored when he published his own tract: Mein Kampf.*"*

"Zhirinovsky clearly represents the worst instincts of Russian chauvinism."

Rabbi Pinchas Goldschmidt, chief rabbi of Moscow

"I'm sure that at least twenty-five percent of the Russians who voted for Zhirinovsky believe in what he says, even if he does not."

"The recent rise of extreme nationalism in Russia due to the economic situation gives us reason enough

to believe that the next president of Russia will be a member of today's opposition—Zhirinovsky or another like him. Therefore, Jews must prepare themselves for the 1996 presidential elections, when Mr. Zhirinovsky or someone else in the opposition might prevail. We must hope for the best but prepare for the worst."

"I'm the last person among Jews in this country to say it but, I fear that in the long term there is no future for the Jew here. I think we must begin to prepare our children for lives outside Russia."

It is obvious from these statements that this author is not the only one who is concerned about the rise of Vladimir Zhirinovsky. There are Zhirinovsky watchers all over the world—all of whom seem to be mad about Vlad (*New York Times*, 2/5/94).

Chapter Twelve

HERE COME THE NEO-FASCISTS

In a February 1994 special report, Gemini News Service reported the following:

> *"The echo of jackboots has been swelling in Europe for several years. Skinhead thugs invoking Adolf Hitler in Germany and Britain were once dismissed as an aberration. France's xenophobic resentment of immigrants has been held in check so far. But now Italy's moderate center has collapsed in a wave of corruption, establishing the old left and a new fascist right as political powers. Worse still, the collapse of the Soviet Union has given rise to a violent new nationalism and a neo-fascist politician, Vladimir Zhirinovsky, who seems to be recapitulating the rise of Hitler and the Nazis."*

From this statement it is obvious that fascist sentiments are welling up all over Europe and Russia. Let's take a closer look at this neo-fascist plague that seems to be sweeping the globe.

HUNGARY

The new prime minister of Hungary is Peter Boross, who is an admirer of Admiral Nicholas Horthy, Hungary's wartime fascist leader.

ITALY

Neo-fascists and communists are collecting most of the votes in Italy's elections as the old Christian democratic order dies in disgrace.

FRANCE

The fascist movement is asserting itself in France with the birth and rapid growth of Jean Marie Le Pens's extreme right-wing National Front Party. Anti-Semitism and anti-black sentiments are growing in France as well.

GERMANY

The same is happening in Germany on an even broader scale. Martin Klingst, reporting for the *Liberal Weekly* in Hamburg, Germany writes:

> "*A pamphlet is spreading fear!* Der Einblick *(Insight), a magazine that circulates among German rightist extremists has printed an article under the headline 'Now It's Time!' The article includes two hundred and fifty names of people from every walk of life—politicians, lawyers, journalists, mayors, social workers, teachers, writers and business people. What they all have in common is a liberal public stance on immigration and refugees and an active stance against the increasing amount of rightist violence occurring in German towns and cities. The magazine did not print these names in order to honor these individuals. For the readers of* Der Einblick, *these people are to blame for the 'wretched condition' that Germany is in today; they are 'enemies' who need to be 'eliminated.' The magazines' goal is clearly enunciated:*

The publisher wants 'the final liquidation of all destructive, anti-German, and anti-nationalist forces in Germany.' The methods to be used are clearly stated— threats, harassment, violence."

GREAT BRITAIN

In Britain these same neo-fascist trends are also on the rise. In an article entitled, "In Britain, A Black Exodus," it is reported that as many as fifty black families per day are applying for emigration status, and most of them want to leave yesterday.

A poll taken in October 1993 showed that ten percent of Her Majesty's subjects would prefer not to live next door to a Jew. And one out of every three Brits would rather not have blacks for neighbors.

It is reported that harassment of ethnic minorities, who represent six percent of the total population is becoming increasingly violent throughout the United Kingdom. In 1992, nine people were killed for purely racist motives and there were an estimated twenty-seven thousand racist attacks.

CONCLUSION

Is history repeating itself? Will fascism once again rear its ugly head in Europe? What about Russia? Is Russia today a reincarnation of the German Weimar republic of the 1930s; and is Vladimir Zhirinovsky a new Hitler poised to take over amidst the chaos? Former Secretary of State James Baker says:

"Democrats and Republicans alike have understood that the threat to Russia is virulent nationalism. It's not a return to communism. I think it's time for everyone to understand that there is a great pos-

sibility of a virulent Russian nationalism becoming much more dominant in Russia" (MacNeil/Lehrer Newshour, 12/14/93).

Let's take a closer look at the striking similarities between Adolf Hitler and Vladimir Zhirinovsky.

Chapter Thirteen

VLAD COMPANY

On December 11, 1993, the day before Russia went to the polls, Yegor Gaidar, leader of the pro-reform and pro-Yeltsin Russia's Choice Party, described the decision facing the voters in these ominous sounding words: *"The choice for Russia is the evolution of Germany after the first world war or after the second world war."*

The very next day, December 12, 1993, Russia's miserable masses vented their frustrations in a right-wing backlash and voted to go back to the first world war. Like Hitler before him, Vladimir Zhirinovsky's popularity was fueled by economic chaos, uncontrolled crime, hyperinflation, national humiliation, a disenfranchised officer class, and a vow to resurrect the empire. By the time the next elections come around Vladimir Zhirinovsky could have something approaching the plurality Hitler received when he became chancellor of Germany in 1933.

The day after the elections, Muscovites went to work with what must have been the political equivalent of a nasty hangover. Dire warnings about the birth of fascism dominated the front pages of newspapers all over the country, while alongside there were reminders of the death four years ago to the very day of Andrei Sakharov, the man perhaps most identified with the struggle for democracy in Russia. *"We are losing his country,"* the caption read. The headlines in one Moscow paper read: *"RUSSIA! THINK ABOUT IT! YOU MUST BE STUPEFIED!"*

The levels of desperation, poverty, crime, confusion, and outright disgust have so deepened that in many people the urge to make a gesture of protest seemed to overpower memory itself. Remember, Russia is a country that lost twenty million people to Nazi Germany in the war and even more to its own totalitarian horrors. However, one voter in four seemed ready not only to risk but to actually invite a repetition. One unidentified man on a Moscow street was reported as saying, *"The people still live in the darkness, and they still want to be deceived."* Another said, *"It's understandable that the less educated people who didn't really understand Zhirinovsky's speeches fell under the spell of his simple tricks."*

ELECTION ANALYSIS

The similarities between the December 1993 Russian election and that held in the German Weimar republic in 1930 are really quite alarming. In the German elections, Heinrich Bruning, Germany's chancellor, was not a politician. In fact, it is said that Bruning was uncomfortable and awkward in front of large crowds. Bruning was uninspiring as he commonly spoke of sacrifices that the German people would need to endure. In similar fashion, Yegor Gaidar, the leader and spokesman for Russia's Choice, the largest of the pro-reform parties, refused to make any populist promises. Instead, he too, like Bruning, spoke of the need for continued sacrifice and patience on the part of the Russian people. Like Bruning before him, Gaidar and his "more pain than gain" campaign was rejected by the voters.

On the December 13, 1994 edition of the *MacNeil/Lehrer Newshour*, David Remnick, a staff writer for *New Yorker* magazine, and Stephen Sestanovich, director of Russian and Eurasian Studies at the Center for Strategic and International Studies in Washington, D.C. discussed the shocking success of Vladimir Zhirinovsky in the Russian parliamentary elections. According to David Remnick, the pro-Yeltsin parties dropped the ball during the campaign:

> *"The pro-reform representatives were terrible on television. They were so boring. They were constantly making the worst sort of academic presentations one can imagine."*

Stephen Sestanovich explains how pro-reformers failed to connect with the pain felt by a majority of Russian voters:

> *"I think it's fair to say that ordinary Russian people were saying that they're hurting too much, and the government party, the pro-democratic party, seemed unresponsive to that hurt. They were not credible on the issue of minimizing the social dislocation. They only kept talking about creating a social safety net but so far there is no social safety net. They seemed heedless of popular concerns. You know, a lot of government figures were saying that they were not going to make any populist appeals during the campaign. I think what that meant to ordinary citizens is we're not promising you anything, we're promising you more hardship."*

During the Weimer republic elections of 1930, Paul von Hindenburg, then German president, stated, *"As a matter of principle, the Reich president should never intervene in an election campaign."* Following in the exact steps of Germany's von Hindenburg, Russian president Boris Yeltsin refused to openly support any one party, preferring to stay above the fray of the campaign. According to David Remnick, this was a strategic error.

> *"Yeltsin must bear a lot of the blame for the re-*

sults here, not only in terms of policy but in his deci-
sion to remain aloof from the campaign, not giving a
vivid endorsement of the Russia's Choice Party. It
turned out to be a disaster because the only very vivid
charismatic politician in the picture became fascist
Vladimir Zhirinovsky."

So as you might expect, the outcomes of the two elections were almost identical. Hitler's Nazi Party who had won only eight hundred and nine thousand votes in 1928, snatched six and a half million votes in 1930 (eighteen percent of the total votes cast). Prior to the December 1993 election, Russian pollsters estimated that Vladimir Zhirinovsky's Liberal Democratic Party would receive no more than two percent of the vote. However, Zhirinovsky surprised everyone and won twenty-five percent of the votes cast for the two hundred and twenty-five seat Duma (the lower house of the new Russian parliament which is filled by proportional representation based on the vote).

I AM NOT A FASCIST

Although Zhirinovsky vehemently denies being a fascist, his party platform tells a completely different story. The Liberal Democratic Party of Zhirinovsky promotes policies of militarism, xenophobia, anti-Semitism, and expansionism—all of which are standard fascist fare. The following is a collection of expert opinions on the question of Zhirinovsky and fascism.

Sergei Gregoriev, deputy press secretary to former Soviet president Mikhail Gorbachev:

"Yes, I would think very much so. I think in many
ways it does remind me of Weimar Germany.

Zhirinovsky is a leader with new charisma, very much reminding me of the notorious Fuhrer of Germany. I would say about Zhirinovsky, that maybe that's an awful definition to call him a Russian fascist. But, he's (1) a nationalist, strong Russian nationalist, and (2) he is very aggressive in terms of his foreign policy. Whether this is enough to make him a fascist, I think it's enough" (*MacNeil/Lehrer Newshour*, 12/13/93).

Jeff Matlock, former U.S. ambassador to Soviet Union; professor of international diplomacy at Columbia University:

"I think there are comparisons there, troubling comparisons that we should not ignore" (*MacNeil/Lehrer Newshour*, 12/13/93).

Stephen Sestanovich, director of Russian and Eurasian studies at the Center for Strategic Studies:

"One of the things that made the rise of Hitler possible was, of course, some accidents of timing, you know. He was actually declining in popularity at the time that he took over. Vladimir Zhirinovsky may very well take advantage of this same type of timing quirk" (*MacNeil/Lehrer Newshour*, 12/13/93).

James Baker, former Secretary of State in the Bush administration:

"If you listen to some of the things that Zhirinovsky has said and if you read some of the things he has written it certainly makes you worry that we are seeing the beginnings of Weimar, Russia. If the reformers do not succeed then that's the direction this thing could go" (*MacNeil/Lehrer Newshour*, 12/14/93).

Derek Ingram, reporter for the Gemini News Service:

"The immediate reaction in Europe to the Russian vote has been a shock that history may be repeating itself. Russia is seen as a reincarnation of the German Weimar republic of the 1920s and Zhirinovsky, a Hitler emerging from the confusion. The immediate chilling visions of Zhirinovsky or his like with a finger on the nuclear button. Alarm bells must be ringing in the Pentagon and alarming scenarios discussed" (World Press Review, 2/94).

Frederick Starr, professor at Oberlin College:

"Zhirinovsky already adopts the full trappings of a tin-horn dictator."

DEJA VU

One of the most striking comparisons between Zhirinovsky and Hitler is found in Zhirinovsky's autobiography. In this book, Zhirinovsky claims that his childhood deprivation and isolation forced him to concentrate on the one overriding idea of his political philosophy: the *"Last Dash to the South."* In this *"last dash,"* Russia would expand its borders by force of arms, back across the newly independent republics of the former Soviet Union, through Turkey, Iran, and Afghanistan all the way to the warm shores of the Indian Ocean. Zhirinovsky says:

"So, the idea emerged of the last 'dash'—last because it will probably be the last repartition of the world. It will be carried out by a newly revived Russian army and it must be carried out in a state of shock therapy, suddenly, swiftly, and effectively."

Like Hitler, Zhirinovsky is known for his tremendous speaking ability. For all practical purposes, Zhirinovsky's speeches are weapons, as much a part of his strategy of conquest as more direct instruments of warfare. In the forward to his autobiography, Zhirinovsky describes himself as a dynamic, a man of great political astuteness, and a magnificent polemicist and speaker. AP correspondent Alan Cooperman says:

> *"Two things happen when Vladimir Zhirinovsky speaks to a Russian audience. First, he is transformed. Then his audience is, too. One-on-one the man known as the frightening fascist and who German newspapers call 'the new Hitler' is cool, calm, and rational. He says he is for peace and nuclear disarmament, against racism and anti-Semitism, and seeks only cooperation with Western Europe, Japan, and the United States. But, you give him an audience, though, and watch him light up the sky. 'President Clinton is a coward.' 'AIDS is a plague from the United States.' 'If Germany and Japan don't stop harassing Russia, bombs will fall on their cities.'"*

Zhirinovsky, like Hitler, has a fascination with the occult. On a recent swing through Eastern Europe Zhirinovsky had an appointment to meet with Bulgaria's most famous psychic, an eighty-year-old woman known as "Baba Vanga."

As we have seen, Zhirinovsky, like Hitler, is strongly anti-Semitic. Also, just as Hitler puts his master plan into book form with his *Mein Kampf*, Zhirinovsky likewise has his *Last Dash to the South*. When one examines the similarities between these two men, it is truly frightening.

Chapter Fourteen

MASTER OF THE MILITARY

One of Vladimir Zhirinovsky's most loyal constituents is the Russian military. In fact, Zhirinovsky may soon be crowned *"Master of the Military"* if his popularity continues to rise. In the December 1993 election, Zhirinovsky received eighty percent of the military vote from units around Moscow. Zhirinovsky also received seventy-two percent of votes cast by Russia's strategic missile forces which control the country's nuclear arsenal. It was also reported that Zhirinovsky's party was the most popular party (receiving eighty-seven percent of the vote) among the Tamad division, one of the key units that helped President Boris Yeltsin crush the October 1993 revolt led by supporters of the elected Soviet-era parliament he had dissolved. The Tamad division was also instrumental in squashing the 1991 coup attempt against then-President Mikhail Gorbachev. It is also reported that police, both secret and civilian, are drawn in large numbers to Zhirinovsky's ultranationalist camp.

Why is Zhirinovsky so popular with the military? It becomes quite clear when one listens to Zhirinovsky's vision for the Russian armed forces.

"I see a proud Russia, a Russia wherein the glorious traditions of its army will once again be realized. This is how I see Russia: It will have the world's strongest army, strategic forces, our missiles with

multiple launchers. Our space combat platforms, our 'Buran' spaceship and 'Energiya' rockets—this is the country's rocket shield. Total security, we have no rival."

According to Jeff Matlock, a former U.S. ambassador to the Soviet Union and now a professor of international diplomacy at Columbia University:

"The military voted for Zhirinovsky because he has the sort of appeal, the simplistic appeal that, well, we simply need to clean out this corruption, we need to use, you know, an iron hand, and this appeals to the mind of many in the military."

Another reason that Zhirinovsky has been able to garner so much military support is because he has promised all active-duty as well as all retired servicemen a rich package of new benefits and incentives. For example, under Zhirinovsky's plan, all military personnel would receive priority status in the areas of housing, business loans, and the allocation of land. Along these same lines, Zhirinovsky has vowed to grant special legal status to all military personnel, including reduced criminal penalties and the right to bear arms and use them in any circumstance. Zhirinovsky has also promised to provide all military officers with a homestead upon retirement. Big Bad Vlad has on many occasions called for more soldiers, more law enforcement officials, and more weapons production. Zhirinovsky says,

"The situation in our country is bad. We are in a big crisis. We need strong government. A strong leader means a strong country."

On December 29, 1993, in what can only be called an attempt to win back the support of a demoralized army,

Russia's defense minister, Pavel Graachev, announced that plans to slash the 2.3 million-strong armed forces to 1.5 million by the year 2000 had been scrapped, and that instead the forces would be cut to 2.1 million by the end of 1994 and remain stable thereafter. Interestingly, Zhirinovsky already has his own paramilitary group, which he calls his Falcons. During the Gulf War Zhirinovsky sent a contingent of his Falcons to fight for Iraqi leader Saddam Hussein. According to Zhirinovsky, these soldiers were sent to *"defend Iraq from its enemies."*

"We [Russia] *have the same enemies as Iraq— America, Israel, and Turkey. America and Israel are both conducting wars against Russia and Iraq."*

CONCLUSION

Zhirinovsky's support seems to have spread all across Russia . . . in cities and in the countryside, and not just among those with a nostalgia for the old empire. Nowhere is this more true than in the ranks of Russia's military. With support like this, Zhirinovsky is an obvious future candidate to succeed President Boris Yeltsin, and should be treated so by the West. As we have seen, Zhirinovsky, like the "Gog" of Ezekiel 38 and 39, has an unquenchable imperial appetite. If Zhirinovsky rises to power in Russia, watch for him to use Russia's military machine to make his imperial ambitions a reality. Consider this quote by Sergei Grigoriantz writing for the *Jerusalem Post* on January 29, 1994:

"The West does not understand the mentality of people like Zhirinovsky and does not take his territorial ambitions seriously. If he comes to power in Russia, Zhirinovsky will begin a war to gain territory, and there will be a threat to the entire civilized world."

Chapter Fifteen

THE MASTER BLASTER

During the 1992 United States presidential campaign, independent candidate Ross Perot took the American political scene by storm. Perot's sharp wit, folksy humor, and penchant for the one-liner made him the people's candidate. Perot was dubbed the "master of the soundbite." Who could forget Perotisms such as, "Let's look under the hood of this thing"; or "If NAFTA is passed there will be a giant sucking sound coming from Mexico."

Like Ross Perot, Vladimir Zhirinovsky is also a master of the soundbite, or is it soundblast? Zhirinovsky's penchant for the bombastic and his ability to both amuse and outrage in the same sentence should soon earn him the title of the *"Master Blaster."* Ariel Cohen, a Salvatori fellow in Russian and Eurasian studies at the Heritage Foundation in Washington, D.C. says: *"Only Adolph Hitler and the Ayatollah Ruhollah Khomeini could compete with Zhirinovsky in the field of bone-chilling declarations."*

Granted, political leaders sometimes lose their cool and make rash statements in the heat of debate or in impromptu settings. But with Zhirinovsky, these rash statements are par for the course. *"He is a master of the bombastic and shocking statement and politically it works,"* says Richard Judy of the Hudson Institute.

> *"Zhirinovsky is a Russian-styled Howard Stern, a foul-mouthed entertainer with a penchant for the politically incorrect and a pathological need for pub-*

lic attention. Zhirinovsky is a feel-good man in a feel-bad era."

"He is like an overgrown class cut-up whose humor has a nasty edge," says Carrol Boget of *Newsweek* magazine.

Zhirinovsky's style has been so successful that even his rivals, the reformers and President Yeltsin himself, are coloring their public speeches with nationalistic sounding rhetoric. For example, on a recent *NBC Nightly News* broadcast, Russian president Boris Yeltsin made the following Zhirinovsky-like statement: *"Russia has the right to act firmly and tough when it is necessary to defend its national interests."*

Most recently, Russian Foreign Minister Andrei Kozyrev (a moderate) gave the *Washington Post* the following Zhirinovsky-sounding comment:

> *"The Kremlin will defend the rights not only of Russians, but of Russian speakers outside the country's borders, and the West must accept Russia's purview in the former Soviet Union as simple reality."*

There can be no doubt that Zhirinovsky has campaigned skillfully as an outsider. He seems to understand that Russians want a see a more aggressive foreign policy and domestic policy, and he is more than happy to oblige. Zhirinovsky spews out verbal Molotov cocktails at every conceivable target. Recently, Vice-President Al Gore cast Zhirinovsky's rhetoric as *"reprehensible and anathema to all freedom-loving people."* As for Zhirinovsky's bombastic, virulent rhetoric, we can only hope and pray that he is as serious as some American political candidates are about their own campaign promises. If this is the case, we have nothing to worry about. However, to those who think that Zhirinovsky is just blowing smoke, listen to Michael McFaul, a research associate at the Center for International Security and Arms Control at Stanford University. McFaul knows all too well that the *"Master Blaster"* is not just a bunch of hot air:

> *"I have followed Zhirinovsky's career very closely since first interviewing him in May of 1991. I have sipped tea with him in the sauna, observed him in action at his party congresses, listened to his oratory on the streets of Moscow, and witnessed his 1991 and 1993 campaigns. In no encounter was I left with the impression that Zhirinovsky was only telling lies to win popular favor, even when he had interest in muting his rhetoric for a Western audience. On the contrary, his sincerity was frightening and disgusting. He is calculating and rational, with a proclivity for sudden, emotional outbursts of rage. This combination keeps his enemies guessing and his followers on edge. It's a quality that makes him a formidable and enduring political player in Moscow, however much Western optimists want him to go away"* (*The New Republic*, 2/14/94).

Chapter Sixteen

THE GOSPEL
ACCORDING TO GOG

In this chapter we will take a closer look at the statements gushing forth from Vladimir Zhirinovsky—this man who would be Gog. From A-Z; from the Alpha to the Omega; this is the gospel according to Gog.

AFGHANISTAN

"There is no such people as the Afghan people."

AFTER HIS RISE TO POWER

"Those who have to be arrested will be arrested quietly at night."

"I will bring the official exchange rate to one ruble to one dollar."

"I recently rejected a one-billion-dollar bribe from a certain Asian country who wanted me to help them get some islands back after I come to power."

"The world should think twice before opposing us, after all, is it really desirable to have a Third World War?"

"I would immediately change the foreign policy radically. In two days, I would do away with countries such as Kazakhstan or Kirghizia. As for the Baltics, I will also cut all

the shipments from Russia—no missile, no timber, no oil, no machinery, and the Lithuanian republic will live for no longer than six months. As you can see, I'm ready to turn both home and foreign policy one hundred percent upside down."

"I will use Russia's greatest resource—its military. I will use the military to enrich the country, be it against Azeris in Russia's farmer markets, Jews in Moscow banks, Ukrainians in Ukraine, or Americans in Alaska."

"Our neighbors will pay Moscow not to redraw borders."

"I will sit down with the United States president and we will divide spheres of influence, with Russia keeping Iran, Turkey, and Afghanistan."

ALASKA

"I will reclaim the forty-ninth U.S. state for Russia."

"I yearn for the day when the Alaskan territory will be returned to the fold of Russia following the breakup of the United States."

ANDROPOV

"He was an uneducated person. There is that stupid little line in his biography: He has higher education. What did that mean? Party correspondence school? Well, what kind of education is that?"

ANTI-SEMITISM

"Although my party is not anti-Semitic, we don't tolerate an increase in the strength of the Jews."

"I envy the Jews because they are the richest nation in

the world."

"I will replace all of Moscow's Jewish television announcers with blue-eyed Russians."

"The Jews were to blame for the first two World Wars and it is they themselves who have provoked anti-Semitism."

"In Russia today, Jewish children are going to school while our children are hungry and forlorn. If you elect me I will put a stop to it."

"Jews, Central Asians, and Armenians and Azerbajanis should be driven from positions of influence. Only people with kind Russian faces should appear on television."

"I myself am not an anti-Semite, but the best outcome would be for a free emigration of Jews out of Russia to Israel."

"No Russian journalist has ever slandered me. The slanderers are in the yellow press, where seventy percent of the staffs are Jewish. They pay dollars to journalists to call me a fascist, an anti-Semite, an anti-Muslim."

"Whenever I am bashed in the press, the article is usually signed by a Jewish name."

"The majority of the new political parties, unfortunately, are headed by Jews, and a Russian Jew is against Russia, because there was anti-Semitism in our country and still is. But we [the Liberal Democratic Party] *are not anti-Semitic."*

"The democratic reforms in Russia have been an Anglo-Saxon and Israeli plan to destroy the Soviet Union."

BALTIC REPUBLICS

"I pledge to reincorporate Latvia, Estonia, and Lithuania

into mother Russia."

"Our goal is to unite Russia in the boundaries of the old Soviet Union, including the Baltic states."

"We will turn them into nuclear waste dumps."

"There will be no Lithuanians, Latvians, or Estonians in the Baltics—I will act as Hitler."

BILL CLINTON

(On President Clinton's decision not to meet with him on a recent visit to Moscow): *"He is afraid that a new honest and brave man has emerged in Russia. But he will not be able to ignore me for long."*

"He is a coward."

"You, Bill Clinton, are my age. You and I belong to the same generation in the same world. America will also soon disintegrate. There too much that is negative has accumulated. There too many problems and inter-ethnic clashes will spring up. Ahead of you lies your own perestroika, your sickness, your degradation. And we Russians will not gloat when some of the states begin to secede, when your plants shut down, when you do not have enough food or medicines, when people start leaving America for Europe, Russia, Japan, South Africa, Australia. We will not gloat when California goes over to Mexico, when a Negro republic is founded in Miami, when the Russians take back Alaska."

CZECHOSLOVAKIA

"The Czechs will be forced to clean the shoes of German officers."

COMMONWEALTH OF INDEPENDENT STATES

"The commonwealth of independent states is nothing but a stillborn child which has no prospect at all of survival."

COMMUNISM

"If we had not started this experiment in October 1917, Russia would a long time ago demanded the greatest powers of the world."

CRIME

"Gang leaders will be arrested and executed on the spot. We will set up courts right on the street and shoot the leaders of criminal bands."

ELIPTON WEAPON

"It has already killed twelve Muslim soldiers in Bosnia."

"I have given the go ahead for the use of the new Elipton weapon by Russian officers in the former Yugoslavia."

"It makes no marks on its victims, leaving only the corpses. There will not be a single trace of firearms wounds, not one drop of blood, not one damaged building."

ETHNIC GROUPS IN MOSCOW

"Dark skinned street vendors in Moscow make it look like a non-Russian city. This is a black stain that should be eradicated."

"News broadcasts on Moscow television should be read only by blond, blue-eyed announcers."

ETHNIC GROUPS IN SOUTHERN RUSSIA

"I will destroy their villages with napalm."

"Like cockroaches, southerners have already spread beyond the Urals. All our problems come from the south."

EXPANSIONISM

"Russia will not move to the west; we have to deal with our southern borders. We will not give away a meter of Russian soil. However, the other way around. . . ."

FAME

"Today the whole world knows about me, not just the whole country—from Kaliningrad to Kamchatka. They know me in Iraq as maybe the closest friend of the Iraqi people. In Finland, conversely, they are afraid of me. They are not too fond of me in Poland, but in Germany they are well disposed; certain political forces in France and South Africa are also sympathetic. I have supporters and opponents in every country of the world."

"I am included among the group of eight leaders of right-wing political parties of the world, along with leaders of Germany, France, Italy, Britain, and Austria. My name is in various directories, there are reports on me by various intelligence services of the world. I am mentioned in correspondence between officials at the highest levels, in reports to the presidents of the world's leading countries."

FOOD SHORTAGES IN RUSSIA

"Russia's shortages of food would end if we simply

stopped feeding the ungrateful republics. "

GERMANY

"We took Berlin in 1945 and gave it back. Now the Germans live well and we live badly. What was the point of taking Berlin? We should have forced millions of Germans to work for us. Then we Russians could have taken things easy. "

In an interview with German radio, Zhirinovsky threatened Germany with what he called a "new Hiroshima" if that country interfered in Russian internal affairs. *"When elected, I will reverse the Russian withdrawal from eastern Germany and move in three hundred thousand troops. "*

"I will take measures to impoverish Germany by exacting more reparations for World War II. "

GORBACHEV

"Gorbachev had an easy life. . . . He was weak because he had it all. He was the son of a landowner. He lived like a little lord even then. He did not have the potential to be a political leader. "

"Gorbachev and Yeltsin bent over backward to help the West, the U.S.A., CIA, and Israel. And what did they get in return? Nothing. Not a thing. They were deceived. Neither the Stavropol bear nor the Ural bear were up to the negotiations. You need a different kind of intellect. . . . What you need here is a person with cosmic intellect, or at least planetary intellect. "

HIS CHILDHOOD

"So all my childhood memories are associated with the

fact that I never had enough to eat. And the food was monotonous and of poor quality. It was the same story with clothing."

"My clothes would be bought at the flea market—from people who had grown out of them, or from dead people. At any rate, the clothes were old and second-hand and belonged to someone else."

"The late arrival of the ambulance at my birth, then a hungry childhood and cold. The winters were harsh, down to minus twenty degrees, but I had poor footwear, I never had warm boots or decent clothes."

"Even in my childhood I felt somehow uncomfortable and unpleasant. I was deprived of the most basic family comfort and human warmth."

"I always had a feeling of a kind of annoyance, bitterness, and dissatisfaction because I never experienced joy . . . any joy. No one fretted over me, no one ever hugged me."

"I grew up in an atmosphere where there was no warmth, not from anyone!"

"My whole life was poverty, I never had money for anything."

HIS LIBERAL DEMOCRATIC PARTY

"We are a moderate party of the right, similar to your Republican Party. You have Duke (speaking of Louisiana's David Duke) as the leader of one of its factions, right? His views are closest to ours."

"Our party represents the Russian people. We are now the leading power. We champion the vital interests of a great Russia. We stand absolutely on a pro-Russia platform. We

strive for a strong and rich Russian state and culture."

HIJ MOTHER

"Two months before her death she said to me: 'Volodya, I have nothing to remember, not one single happy day.' And when she died in May 1985 I looked back over her life and I felt so bad that she had indeed experienced no joy. Nothing but humiliation and suffering all her life."

HIJ PAJJION FOR GEOGRAPHY

"At an early age I was attracted by other countries, I knew what the continents were, I loved geography lessons. I was also attracted to politics, philosophy, economics, foreign policy, social problems, the nationalities question—I had already somehow experienced all this for myself in practice. Eventually I mastered everything."

"I applied myself with frenzy to my studies."

"My disadvantaged personal life helped make me a good student. I tried to find some sort of satisfaction from this, and I graduated with distinction from the Institute of Asian and African Countries."

IRAQ

"We ought to be willing to blow up a few Kuwaiti ports and aircraft, plus a few American ships to defend an old Soviet ally, Iraq."

"I have met with Saddam Hussein, who for two years after the war, received no foreigners at all, least of all Russians. Deputies from the Russian parliament, leaders of various parties, and journalists went to see him, but he received

only me in November of 1992. We talked for four hours in his palace in Baghdad."

KAZAKHSTAN

"Why should we Russians give a space program to the Kazakhs? They're camel shepherds for Christ sake. They want to live without electricity, they prefer yurts, they like that smell."

"If those Muslim chumps want to sit around and count their worry beads, I say let them. No reason to give them nuclear weapons."

KHRUSHCHEV

"He was the same as Gorbachev. He graduated from the 'Red' academy. He had absolutely no education in the humanities."

LITHUANIA

"I'll bury radioactive waste along the Lithuanian border and put up powerful fans and blow the stuff across at night. They'll all get radiation sickness. They'll die of it. When they either die out or get down on their knees, I'll stop."

NEW AGE RHETORIC

"When I worked for the Committee for the Defense of Peace, I worked abroad. I had contacts with foreign delegations from Western Europe and America. I helped prepare international congresses—and eventually my planetary outlook began to emerge. We are all citizens of the same planet."

"*Politics, which involves the lives of millions of people, is the most responsible of jobs. You could not think up anything more responsible. Even the defense minister has less responsibility. He only has the armed forces. But here you have the whole country. And sometimes the whole planet. Because a great thermonuclear power like Russia, or America, or China, means making decisions on a planetary scale.*"

"*What is needed here is a man who thinks on a cosmic scale, at the very least a planetary scale. Then a result could be achieved which would lead to a reasonable kind of existence and the implementation of a geopolitical formula to ensure the interests of the majority of the planet.*"

ON THE RELEASE OF HARD-LINERS RUTSKOI AND KHASBULATOV

"*Well done guys, this is our day today. When Russia chooses her next president the choice will be between me and Rutskoi (former vice-president and Afghan war hero).*"

"*We should fill their now vacant cells with Yeltsin and his chief advisors.*"

PAST RUSSIAN LEADERS

"*Vladimir Lenin's rule was like rape. Stalin's period was a period of homosexuality. Krushchev's epoch was masturbation. Brezhnev's era was group sex. Yeltsin's rule is political and economic impotence.*"

"*All Russia's rulers have lacked a classical education.*"

POLITICAL CATCH PHRASES

"*Throw out the foreigners!*"

"Restore the Old Empire!"

"I want to make Russia great again!"

"Let us make others suffer!"

The motto present on all of Zhirinovsky's campaign posters reads: *"I will bring Russia up off Her knees!"*

"We are going to get it back! Whatever we had, we are going to get it back!"

"The Russian people have three choices. We can either choose what we have now by voting for the reform leaders, or we can choose to go backward by voting for the communists. My party represents the third choice."

"Russia has suffered enough, first under seventy years of communism and then two years under shock therapy imposed by the imperialism of the International Monetary Fund and the World Bank."

POLITICAL FUTURE

In February 1994 Zhirinovsky told ten thousand cheering supporters in Montenegro (the only republic remaining with Serbia in the Yugoslav federation), *"Wait just a little longer and we will change our government and leadership in Moscow."*

"I say it quite plainly, when I come to power there will be a dictatorship."

"I am waiting in the wings; my moment has nearly arrived."

"Today is the beginning of orgasm," Zhirinovsky told reporters as he cast his ballot in the December 1993 elections. *"The whole nation, I promise you, will experience or-*

gasm next year!"

"It" (speaking of his possible election as president in 1996) *"would be a splendid fiftieth birthday present for me."*

When asked in 1991 how he had leaped from political obscurity to win six million votes in the Russian republic's presidential election, Zhirinovsky stated: *"I promised to defend Russians. Until I came along nobody dared to use this slogan. But now nationalists have come to power in the Caucasus, Central Asia, the Ukraine, the Baltic states, Moldavia. Whether people like it or not, the same processes will soon begin in Russia itself."*

"I know a significant percentage of the Russian people are behind me. If Russian presidential elections were held today, I would have a good chance of winning. About forty million voters may vote for me."

"Voting papers for the election of president were distributed during the December parliamentary election as a poll and twenty-nine percent voted for me. The remaining candidates, Yeltsin included, did not even get ten percent each. What better proof could there be? I received five or six times more votes than any other candidate."

ROMANIA

"Romania is nothing but an artificial state created by Italian gypsies who seized territory from Russia, Bulgaria, and Hungary."

RUSSIA

"Russia? This is a historical name, it is a geographical

concept. It does not by any means denote a state for Russians. It is the Eurasian continent. It is twenty-two million square kilometers. It is the Arctic Ocean which washes our northern borders. It is the Pacific Ocean in the Far East. It is the Atlantic, via the Black and Baltic Seas. And in the future the Indian Ocean, when we have accomplished our final 'southern dash.'"

"I see a proud Russia, a Russia wherein the glorious traditions of its army will once again be realized."

"This is how I see Russia: It will have the world's strongest army, strategic forces, our missiles with multiple launchers. Our space combat platforms, our 'Buran' spaceship and 'Energiya' rockets—this is the country's rocket shield. Total security, we have no rival."

"To this day Russia has not received adequate compensation from the Germans, from the French, from the Japanese, from the Swedes, from the Turks, from the Poles—from a single one of the aggressors who have trampled and destroyed our country."

"The world should be grateful to Russia for its role as savior. And this is not Russia's reward for the troubles it has borne in fulfilling its historic mission every hundred years. It is Russia's natural development. It is its awakening and its ability once again to help the peoples of the south to gain true liberation, that the hour of silence may come at last in the Near and Middle East, in Asia Minor, and Central Asia. Only Russia can help here."

"Today Russians are being told in some places: 'Get out of here; you're occupiers, you're colonizers!' When it was Russians who gave everything to those nations and raised them from primitive societies to the space age! We brought them to outer space, and they're spitting in Russians' faces."

SERBIA

"If I come to power I will order three hundred thousand Russian troops to the Balkans to back the Serbs."

"The West is trying to kill Serbs as a part of a plot to encircle Russia with a green Muslim corridor."

"A Third World War against the Slavs and the Orthodox faith has already been unleashed on the sly, and it is being instigated by the United States, Germany, and the Catholic Vatican."

"U.N. sanctions against Serbia should be lifted."

"Any attack on Russia's Serb brothers is an attack on Russia. It would be the same as declaring war on Russia."

"I will unseat the current government in Moscow and help warring Serbs resist the West."

"Russia has a historic role to stop the Western attacks on our Orthodox Serb brothers."

THE YEAR 1994

"1993 is the last year of delay, instability, uncertainty. In 1994, progress in a positive direction will begin. For sure, we will be able after all to form a new political leadership and establish a new concept as the foundation of all areas of our domestic and foreign policy."

In February 1994 Zhirinovsky predicted that his Liberal Democratic Party *"may definitely come to power this year."*

THE YEAR 2000

"Russians, proud people, the twenty-first century will

belong to us despite everything! In the next seven years we will finally stop all revolutions, all perestroikas, all the Gorbystroikas, we will put an end to Yeltsinism. . . ."

"We will enter the twenty-first century changed and pure. Right now we are in the bath. We are washing away the scabs, the dirt that has accumulated throughout the twentieth century. That is bad. But clearly even this was necessary to us, to our sorrowful country, in order to finally wash away the contagion, the satanic infection, that afflicted us in the early century, that was unloosed on central Russia from the West in order to poison the country and undermine it from within. . . . We will put an end to this. We will emerge as the most fire-hardened nation."

"We must end all wars by the end of the twentieth century and enter the third millennium with only minor private conflicts."

TURKEY

"What culture did the Turks ever bring to the territory of Asia Minor? There is no such thing as Turkish culture, culture does not go with the bare saber."

"The Turks have brought as much evil upon mankind as the Germans. But the Germans, their party, their ideology, were put on trial. But nobody punished the Turks."

"Nothing would happen in the world even if the whole Turkish nation perished."

UKRAINE

"I don't want to hear anything about the independent Ukraine. Never ever should they have their own currency

called the grevna. Never ever will there be such a thing as the Ukrainian navy. There is no such thing. I will turn everything towards Russia."

UNITED STATES

Zhirinovsky has repeatedly said that the only things America ever gave the world were chewing gum and AIDS. He has also urged American visitors to set up a "Martin Luther King Republic" in the middle of the United States, with Michael Jackson as president and Angela Davis as vice-president.

"The United States is the empire of evil."

"The only reason Americans come to Russia with foreign aid is to scan the territory to decide where they will drop their bombs."

"We shall not allow you Americans to pump our resources out of our land and give us pantyhoses, Coca-Cola, and McDonald's instead."

"You, the Americans, have awarded Shevardnadze with the title of doctor of political science. His place is in prison and you promote him to become the world's politician, so you are participating in the disintegration of Russia. So if I become president one day, I would take into consideration the fact that our country is feeling strong against the Americans."

"In the future we can help you in many ways because I know that you're feeling the pressure of the overall structure of the population being changed. More Hispanics and blacks are living in your country today than there used to be. What I mean is, I've been to New York, I have seen no white America at all. The blacks are all over the place. You're running a

serious risk of the key positions in the political and economic life of the country being eventually seized by the blacks and the Hispanics. White America may be at the verge of a disappearance. You can end up being turned into a second sort of people. So in this way, a union between the U.S.A., Germany, and Russia could have contributed to the preservation of the white race on the European and American continents."

"Americans remain the last nation, the last people, the last state, that still makes a noise, that still sends in its quick reaction forces, that imposes its will on Iraq, Libya, Serbia. Leave these people in peace. Do not interfere in the affairs of Europe, Asia, Africa, Latin America, Australia. Look after your own problems. Do not tell us what to do in the Baltics, in Central Asia, in the Dniester region, in the Transcaucasus. And we will not tell you what to do in the southern states, or ask why you kidnapped the legitimate president of Panama; why you sent a landing force to the island of Grenada. A time will come when you will have to answer for it."

"I will beat the Americans in space. I will surround the planet with our space stations so that they will be scared of our space weapons."

"America's days are numbered. Sometime in the next century the population of the U.S. will perish, swamped by blacks and Hispanics, the U.S. will go the way of the USSR."

U.S.—RUSSIA SPY SCANDAL

"A normal thing that happens sometimes, like a railway catastrophe."

WHY POLITICS?

"All these factors seemed to be coming on top of each

other. My unhappy childhood, the lack of good friends, poor everyday living conditions, bad food, poor leisure, non-party status, the fact that I had lived in various regions—all this was the foundation on which my political identity began to mature. If I had been born in an affluent family in a Russian city, among Russian people, and had never moved anywhere, if my childhood friends and the girl I loved had been right there next to me, then maybe I would have turned my back on politics."

ZHIRINOVSKY'S "LAST DASH TO THE SOUTH"

"I long to swim naked in the Indian Ocean."

"I advocate the conquest of Afghanistan, Iran, and Turkey and the occupation of the Persian Gulf and the Mediterranean."

"I dream of Russian soldiers washing their boots in the warm waters of the Indian Ocean and switching to summer uniforms: forever. Lightweight boots, short-sleeved, open-necked shirts with no tie, lightweight trousers, lightweight caps. And a small, modern Russian assault rifle produced by the Izhevsk plant."

"All this will become possible if we take this last 'dash' south. We badly need this, it is medicine that we must take."

"We should either emerge onto the shores of the Pacific and Indian Oceans, or cut the south off from us behind a 'Great Wall of China.' But in the latter case, our trade ties with Iran and Turkey and with Afghanistan would deteriorate. This would make us poorer. We clearly cannot countenance this. So there is only one option. We must carry out this operation code-named the 'last dash south.'"

"Our army will perform this task. This will be a method

of ensuring the survival of the nation as a whole, it will be the renaissance of the Russian army. New armed forces can be reborn only as a result of a combat operation. The army cannot grow stronger in military commissariats and barracks. It needs a goal, a task."

"Russia's soldiers will once again stand guard over the nineteen borders of the Soviet Union, and once we have put them there, they will not move back a single step."

"All Russia has to do is sit back and wait for ethnic and national conflicts from the Caucasus Mountains to Asia to rage out of control, and then the West will pass us, the Russians, to save the remnants of millions of people in those countries."

"The last dash to the south, Russia's outlet to the shores of the Indian and Mediterranean Ocean, is really the task of saving Russia."

"All Russia's problems are in the south. So until we resolve our southern problem we will never extricate ourselves from the protracted crisis, which will periodically worsen."

"So, the idea emerged of the last 'dash'—last because it will probably be the last repartition of the world and it must be carried out in a state of shock therapy, suddenly, swiftly, and effectively."

"We will gain a four-zone platform. When we can rest on the Arctic Ocean in the north, the Pacific Ocean in the east, and the Atlantic via the Black, Mediterranean, and Baltic Seas, and finally, when we can rest on the shores of the Indian Ocean in the south like a huge pillar, we will also gain friendly neighbors. Enmity will cease forever."

"We must ensure stability throughout our region for Russia, and the world community as a whole. This is historically

natural, it is not an invention, not fantasy. It is reality. We stand on the south but it is unstable, it is ablaze, it is in revolt. The Afghan tribes, the Turkmens, the Azerbaijanis, the Tajiks, the Armenians, and the Iranian tribes, they are all in a state of open warfare and hostility. And since these peoples have often fought, they now have a blood feud, they can no longer calm down, they will always fight. But mankind cannot allow constant war in the south of Russia. These wars in the Near East will not end and may eventually trigger World War III."

"Russia's last dash to the south will also preclude World War III. It is not only the solution to Russia's internal problems and the pacification of the peoples of this region. It is also the resolution of a global task, of planetary significance. America, too, will have tranquility because wars have ended in this region and there are no Red, or Muslim, or Turkic, or Islamic fundamentalist threats. Tasks of geopolitical significance will be resolved."

"The idea of the last 'dash' to the south is noble, it entails only positive consequences. However, despite everything, this is a method of treatment, and it is possible that someone may have a negative reaction. But this is the solution of world problems, and not everyone can be happy."

"We must reach agreement, and let it be a world treaty to the effect that we divide up the whole planet and spheres of economic influence operating in a north-south direction. First, Japan and China go south into southeast Asia, the Philippines, Indonesia, and Australia. Second, Russia can go south into Afghanistan, Iran, and Turkey. Third, Western Europe can go south into the African continent. Fourth, and finally, North America and Canada can go south into the whole of Latin America. This is all on equal terms. No one has any advantages here. The direction is the same—southward."

"The allocation according to this geopolitical model would be beneficial for all mankind. Warm, clear weather would be established over the entire planet. Cloudless weather, without hurricanes and storms."

"The pros of carrying out this operation considerably outweigh the cons which may naturally be perceived. The Russian army needs this so that our guys can flex their muscles, tired as they are of 'hazing' instead of sitting around in barracks, in the depths of Russia, waiting for the end of their term of service, not knowing where the enemy is, who the adversary is, or what is needed to prepare themselves morally and physically. This would be a cleansing for us all."

"The southern campaign. . . . Once, the Red Cavalry was marching on Warsaw, and this was the slogan: 'Forward, to the English Channel—On to Warsaw, Berlin, the Channel.' Then our cavalry, moving to the east, reached the Pacific Ocean, where their march ended. In 1979-89 the Red Army went down to Afghanistan. At one time, in 1919, only the Entente stopped its (the cavalry's) progress and the taking of Constantinople. And in 1916 the Russians reached the Iraqi border. And they were in northern Iran for many years, until 1946, I think. So, the advance to the south is nothing new for Russia. This is a normal direction of movement for Russia."

"Russia will do what is foreordained and will fulfill the great historical mission—liberate the world from wars, which always begin in the south."

"This operation—the last 'dash' south—is not the Barbarossa plan (Hitler's plan for the invasion of Russia), not Napoleon's plans, not the military ventures of Swedish King Charles XII. It is purely a Russian variant, it has been elaborated by Russia's very fate. Otherwise, Russia will be unable to develop and will perish."

"We must accomplish this surge of ours to the south, this last campaign, in order once and for all to put an end to the danger on the Fatherland's southern borders and to help the peoples who are Russia's neighbors gain a peaceful life and eliminate hotbeds of war and tension, which lead to conflicts."

"The Russian army will assemble for the last time for its southern campaign and will stop forever on the shores of the Indian Ocean. Beyond that there is nowhere to go."

"A great historical mission has fallen to Russia. It may be its last."

"Russia must therefore go south and reach the shores of the Indian Ocean. This is not just my whim. It is Russia's destiny. It is a fate. It is Russia's great exploit. We must do it, because we have no choice. There is no other way for us. It is geopolitics. Our development demands it, like a child who has outgrown his clothes and must put on new ones."

"Let Russia successfully accomplish its last dash to the south. I see Russian soldiers gathering for this last southern campaign. I see Russian commanding officers in the headquarters of Russian divisions and armies, sketching the lines of march of troop formations and the end points of their marches. I see planes at air bases in the southern districts of Russia. I see submarines surfacing off the shores of the Indian Ocean and landing craft approaching the shores, where soldiers of the Russian army are already marching, infantry combat vehicles are advancing, and vast numbers of tanks are on the move. Russia is at last accomplishing its final military campaign."

CONCLUSION

These statements sound like they came straight from the

pages of Ezekiel 38 and 39 and straight from the mouth of the man who would be Gog! These are the kind of statements that leave Zhirinovsky's followers crying for more. Such statements delight and excite many millions of Russians helping them in an almost therapeutic way to release deep-felt resentment and to soothe their wounded pride. Zhirinovsky's seemingly endless stream of bombastic rhetoric corresponds to the demands and despair felt by the Russian people. Zhirinovsky is definitely scratching where the Russian people itch.

Chapter Seventeen

THE LAST DASH TO THE SOUTH

As we have seen in earlier chapters, the Word of God declares that in the last days a power-crazed ruler referred to cryptically as *"Gog"* will lead a massive invasion into the land of Israel. In the last chapter we saw that Zhirinovsky's political manifesto is entitled *Last Dash to the South* and that a southern military campaign into Central Asia and the Middle East is his ultimate goal. This is precisely what Ezekiel 38 and 39 describe. It will indeed be Gog's "last dash to the south." In chapter one we looked at the participants in this invasion. Let's now take a closer look at the outcome of the invasion.

EASY PICKENS

The Bible tells us that at the time of Gog's attack, Israel will be residing in her land unprotected and apparently not expecting a military onslaught of this magnitude. God refers to Israel in Ezekiel 38:11 as a land of *"unwalled villages,"* a land which is *"at rest and living securely."* From all outward appearances, Gog and his marauding band will enjoy an easy victory. However, one must not forget that God is in ultimate control. In fact, the Bible tells us that God Himself is orchestrating the whole scenario. We read in Ezekiel 38:4,8,16:

> *"And I will turn thee back, and put hooks into thy*

jaws, and I will bring thee forth, and all thine army . . . After many days thou shalt be visited . . . it shall be in the latter days, and I will bring thee against my land. . . ."

God brings Gog into the land of Israel in order to bring glory to Himself. The Bible says in Ezekiel 38:16, 23:

". . . I will bring thee against my land, that the heathen may know me, when I shall be sanctified in thee, O Gog, before their eyes. . . . Thus will I magnify myself, and sanctify myself; and I will be known in the eyes of many nations, and they shall know that I am the LORD."

FIGHTING MAD

As the forces of Gog invade Israel they will appear invincible. But God will supernaturally intervene on behalf of His people. The Bible says that as the hordes of Gog enter the land that God's wrath will well up within Him.

"And it shall come to pass at the same time when Gog shall come against the land of Israel, saith the Lord GOD, that my fury shall come up in my face. For in my jealousy and in the fire of my wrath have I spoken . . ." (Ezek. 38:18–19).

The Bible tells us that God will use a four-pronged attack to decimate Gog and his invading forces on the mountains of Israel. Let's examine each element of God's supernatural arsenal.

SHAKE, RATTLE, AND ROSH

The first means God uses to destroy Gog and his confederation is a massive earthquake. The Bible tells us in Ezekiel 38:19–20:

> "For in my jealousy and in the fire of my wrath have I spoken, Surely in that day there shall be a great shaking in the land of Israel; So that the fishes of the sea, and the fowls of the heaven, and the beasts of the field, and all creeping things that creep upon the earth, and all the men that are upon the face of the earth, shall shake at my presence, and the mountains shall be thrown down, and the steep places shall fall, and every wall shall fall to the ground."

This passage clearly tells us that there will be a "whole lotta shakin' goin' on" in the day of Gog's invasion of Israel. In that day God will send an earthquake of enormous magnitude to strike down the invading army of Gog with a permanent case of "Richter mortis."

BACK STABBERS

The second means that God will use to destroy Gog will be infighting and chaos among the invading troops. The Bible makes this very clear in Ezekiel 38:21:

> "And I will call for a sword against him [Gog] throughout all my mountains, saith the Lord GOD: every man's sword shall be against his brother."

No doubt when the earthquake strikes, the forces of Gog will become disoriented and confused and they will break rank and begin to lash out at one another. It is important to remember that Gog's strike force will be composed of troops from many different nations (i.e., Russia, Turkey, Iran, Egypt, Sudan, Libya, and the Moslem nations of Central Asia). In the post-earthquake pandemonium, communications between the invading forces will break and the soldiers will begin killing anyone who does not speak their language. This will no doubt be the worst case of death by *friendly fire* ever recorded.

DEATH IN EPIDEMIC PROPORTIONS

The third means that God will employ to decimate Gog is pestilence or plagues. The Word of God says: *"And I will plead against him with pestilence and with blood . . ."* (Ezek. 38:22).

Interestingly, this word "pestilence" is the exact same Hebrew word used in Exodus 9:3 of the deadly plague that struck Pharaoh's livestock. Therefore, it would seem clear that in that day God will visit Gog and his armies with a similar plague. This plague will simply compound the pain and destruction that will already be present.

FIRE AND ICE

The fourth and final method that God will use to annihilate Gog will be with a torrential downpour of rain mixed with hail, fire, and brimstone. The Bible says in Ezekiel 38:22: *". . . and I will rain upon him, and upon his bands, and upon the many people that are with him, an overflowing rain, and great hailstones, fire, and brimstone."*

In what can only be described as an instant replay of Sodom and Gomorrah, God utterly destroys Gog and his hordes with a supernatural cloudburst of fire and ice. But that's not all! God not only destroys Gog and his armies with this fire, but He also will send this same firestorm to rain down destruction on Gog's homeland of Magog as well. Listen to the Word of God:

"And I will send a fire on Magog, and among them

that dwell carelessly in the isles: and they shall know that I am the LORD" (Ezek. 39:6).

The scope of the destruction described here is massive. Millions of people will be wiped off the face of the earth by this fiery torrent of hail, brimstone, and rain.

GOG R.I.P.

The destruction of Gog is not the end of the story. The Word of God goes on in Ezekiel 39:4–24 to describe the gruesome aftermath of Gog's annihilation. Here we read that the calm after the storm of God's judgment is filled with two activities:

1. The burial of the dead
2. The feeding of the birds of the air and the beasts of the field on the carrion.

The enormous extent of the carnage can be seen by the fact that it takes seven months to bury all the corpses of those slain. The burial is necessary in order to cleanse the land. The Word of God says:

> *"And it shall come to pass in that day, that I will give unto Gog a place there of graves in Israel, the valley of the passengers on the east of the sea: and it shall stop the noses of the passengers: and there shall they bury Gog and all his multitude: and they shall call it The valley of Hamon-gog. And seven months shall the house of Israel be burying of them, that they may cleanse the land"* (Ezek. 39:11–12).

In this passage the Bible tells us that the number of corpses buried is so great that the name of the valley where the burial takes place will be changed to "Hamon-gog," which translated means "the valley of the hordes of Gog." It is ironic that the only piece of land that Gog will seize in the land of Israel will be his own burial plot. Gog, whose master plan it was to bury Israel is himself the one who ends up being buried.

THE BIRDS

The second event that occurs after God's destruction of Gog is almost too gruesome to mention. The Bible tells us that the slaughter of the hordes of Gog will provide a veritable smorgasbord for the birds of the air and the beasts of the field. God refers to this carnage simply as *"My sacrifice"* or *"My table."* In other words, God sends out an open invitation to the birds and the beasts to eat their fill as His guests.

> *"Thou shalt fall upon the mountains of Israel, thou . . . and the people that is with thee: I will give thee unto the ravenous birds of every sort, and to the beasts of the field to be devoured. Thou shalt fall upon the open field: for I have spoken it, saith the Lord GOD. . . . And, thou son of man, thus saith the Lord GOD; Speak unto every feathered fowl, and to every beast of the field, Assemble yourselves, and come; gather yourselves on every side to my sacrifice that I do sacrifice for you, even a great sacrifice upon the mountains of Israel, that ye may eat flesh, and drink blood. Ye shall eat the flesh of the mighty, and drink the blood of the princes of the earth, of rams, of lambs, and of goats, of bullocks, all of them fatlings of Bashan. And ye shall eat fat till ye be full, and drink blood till ye be drunken, of my sacrifice which I have sacrificed for you. Thus ye shall be filled at my table with horses and chariots, with mighty men, and with all men of war, saith the Lord GOD"* (Ezek. 39:4–5,17–20).

What a picture of utter humiliation and degradation this is! Gog and his entire army are slain and then given over as a sacrifice to the birds of the air and the beasts of the field.

CONCLUSION

As we have seen, the Word of God declares that in the last days a power-crazed leader that the Bible refers to cryptically as "Gog" will lead a massive invasion south into the land of Israel. This man, like Vladimir Zhirinovsky, will possess the following attributes:

- He will come from an area far to the north of Israel (38:6,15)
- He will be from the land of Magog (38:2)
- He will be the prince of Rosh or Russia (38:2)
- He will be strongly anti-Semitic (38:9,14)
- He will have a desire to conquer and plunder Israel (38:11-14)
- He will have an insatiable imperial appetite (38:11)
- He will see Israel as a land of great wealth and riches (38:11-14)
- He will arise in the last days (38:8,16)
- He will have an evil plan (38:10)
- He will lead a mighty army on an ill-fated "final dash to the south" (38:4)

Is Vladimir Volfovich Zhirinovsky the man who would be Gog? You be the judge!

Chapter Eighteen

THE GOSPEL ACCORDING TO GOD

One of the reasons I love to study the Bible so much is because it is a book filled with prophecy. Through the prophetic passages of the Bible, God shows us again and again that He alone is the author and controller of history. History is indeed His story! For the Christian, prophecy should produce "fruits." They are as follows:

WORSHIP

A clear understanding of God's plan for the future gives us insight into the wisdom, knowledge, power, and majesty of God. The Bible speaks to this in Romans 11:33-36:

> *"O the depth of the riches both of the wisdom and knowledge of God! how unsearchable are his judgments, and his ways past finding out! For who hath known the mind of the Lord? or who hath been his counsellor? Or who hath first given to him, and it shall be recompensed unto him again? For of him, and through him, and to him, are all things: to whom be glory for ever. Amen."*

COMFORT

A clear understanding of God's prophetic plan ought to

bring encouragement and comfort to those of us who have placed our trust in Jesus Christ. As we go through the trials of life, it is a comfort to know that an all-powerful God has a plan for our universe, and it cannot be thwarted. This same God also has a plan for our individual lives as well.

The Apostle Paul, writing to the church at Thessalonica concerning the events on God's prophetic calendar, writes:

"Wherefore comfort one another with these words" (1 Thess. 4:18).

"Wherefore comfort yourselves together, and edify one another, even as also ye do" (1 Thess. 5:11).

STABILITY

A clear understanding of God's prophetic plan for the future ought to help us remain steady and sure. As the world around us becomes more chaotic and difficult to understand we should look for direction and stability in God's prophetic Word. By doing so we will not fall prey to panic or fear. Once again the Apostle Paul speaks to this point:

> *"Now we beseech you, brethren, by the coming of our Lord Jesus Christ, and by our gathering together unto him, That ye be not soon shaken in mind, or be troubled, neither by spirit, nor by word, nor by letter as from us, as that the day of Christ is at hand"* (2 Thess. 2:1–2).

HOLINESS

A clear understanding of God's prophetic plan for the future gives us an incentive to live holy and pure lives. Knowing that a day of judgment is indeed coming should motivate us to live blamelessly before the Lord. Therefore, prophecy should produce holiness. The Bible makes this clear in 2 Peter 3:10-12:

> *"But the day of the Lord will come as a thief in the night; in the which the heavens shall pass away with a great noise, and the elements shall melt with fervent heat, the earth also and the works that are therein shall be burned up. Seeing then that all these things shall be dissolved, what manner of persons ought ye to be in all holy conversation and godliness, Looking for and hasting unto the coming of the day of God, wherein the heavens being on fire shall be dissolved, and the elements shall melt with fervent heat?"*

For the non-Christian, prophecy should produce a healthy fear and reverential awe of God. This same God who controls world rulers and world events also controls the ultimate destiny of your soul. As the non-Christian sees the events described in the Word of God coming to pass, there ought to be a desire to get right with God before it is too late.

Once again the Bible provides us with the essential steps for getting right with God. The steps are as simple as A-B-C.

A

Acknowledge that you are a sinner!

"For whosoever shall keep the whole law, and yet offend in one point, he is guilty of all" (Jam. 2:10).

"For all have sinned, and come short of the glory of God" (Rom. 3:23).

"For the wages of sin is death; but the gift of God is eternal life through Jesus Christ our Lord" (Rom. 6:23).

B

Believe upon the Lord Jesus Christ!

"But God commendeth his love toward us, in that, while we were yet sinners, Christ died for us" (Rom. 5:8).

"For he hath made him to be sin for us, who knew no sin; that we might be made the righteousness of God in him" (2 Cor. 5:21).

"I said therefore unto you, that ye shall die in your sins: for if ye believe not that I am he, ye shall die in your sins" (John 8:24).

"That which is born of the flesh is flesh; and that which is born of the Spirit is spirit" (John 3:6).

C

Come to Christ today!

"All that the Father giveth me shall come to me; and him that cometh to me I will in no wise cast out" (John 6:37).

"For he saith, I have heard thee in a time accepted, and in the day of salvation have I succoured thee: behold, now is the accepted time; behold, now is the day of salvation" (2 Cor. 6:2).

It is my prayer that God would use this book to encourage believers in Jesus Christ, and draw those who are presently outside the Kingdom of God to a saving faith in Christ.

Chapter Nineteen

CHRONOLOGY OF RECENT MAJOR EVENTS IN RUSSIA

AUGUST 1991

Communist hardliners attempt a coup in Moscow to oust Mikhail Gorbachev from power. After three days, the coup fails and Gorbachev is for a brief period returned to power.

SEPTEMBER 1991

Civil war breaks out in the Georgia republic.

DECEMBER 8, 1991

Leaders of Russia, Byelorussia, and Ukraine meet in the Byelorussian city of Brest to declare the end of the U.S.S.R.

DECEMBER 17, 1991

Mikhail Gorbachev and Boris Yeltsin meet in Moscow to discuss an orderly transition of power. They agree that the Soviet Union would cease to exist by 1992.

DECEMBER 21, 1991

Eleven former Soviet republics meet in the Kazakh city

of Alma-Ata (ironically the birthplace of ultranationalist Vladimir Zhirinovsky) and sign an agreement to create a commonwealth.

DECEMBER 23, 1991

Gorbachev and Yeltsin meet again in the Kremlin to discuss the final transfer of power.

DECEMBER 25, 1991

Gorbachev officially resigns as president of the Soviet Union. Boris Yeltsin is elected president of Russia. Placing third in the ballot (six million votes) is Vladimir Zhirinovsky.

DECEMBER 31, 1991

The Soviet flag atop the Kremlin is officially replaced by the red, white, and blue flag of pre-revolutionary Russia.

FEBRUARY 1, 1992

George Bush meets at Camp David with Boris Yeltsin. The two leaders declare an end to the Cold War and outline guidelines for future relations between the U.S. and Russia.

FEBRUARY 1992

Uzbekistan, Turkmenistan, Tajikistan, and Kirghizia join together with Iran, to form an Islamic commonmarket.

SEPTEMBER 1993

Vladimir Zhirinovsky publishes his autobiography which

is apocalyptically entitled *Last Dash to the South.*

OCTOBER 1993

Boris Yeltsin dissolves the Russian Parliament and hard-liners led by Alexander Rutskoi, barricade themselves in the Russian Parliament building. One hundred and forty people were killed. This was the worst instance of political violence in Moscow since the 1917 Bolshevik Revolution.

DECEMBER 1, 1993

In a presidential decree, Boris Yeltsin replaced the hammer and sickle with the two-headed Romanov eagle as the official government seal of the new Russia.

DECEMBER 12, 1993

Russia holds its first free multiparty elections since the 1917 Revolution. Vladimir Zhirinovsky's Liberal Democratic Party receives twenty-five percent of the sixty million votes cast, the most of any party.

Vladimir Zhirinovsky
and the
Last Dash
to the South

Mark Hitchcock and Scot Overbey

"Let Russia successfully accomplish its last 'dash' to the South. I see Russian soldiers gathering for this last southern campaign. I see Russian commanding officers in the headquarters of Russian divisions and armies, sketching the lines of troop movements. . . . I see planes at airbases in the southern districts of Russia. I see submarines surfacing off the shores of the Indian Ocean and landing crafts approaching shores where soldiers of the Russian army are already marching. . . . Infantry combat vehicles are advancing and vast numbers of tanks are on the move. Russia is at last accomplishing its final military campaign."

Is this a paraphrase of Ezekiel 38 and 39? NO! It is a quotation from Vladimir Zhirinovsky's book, *Last Dash to the South*. This is a remarkable video. Nothing you have seen or read will impress you, your friends, and your fellow Church members like this presentation.

Hitler foretold his plans in *Mein Kampf.* The world laughed. Likewise, Zhirinovsky has foretold his plans in his autobiography. This video documents Zhirinovsky's "evil thought" toward Israel (Ezekiel 38:10).

Actual news footage of Vladimir Zhirinovsky

ISBN 1-879366-73-8   **48 minute video**

Also Available from
Hearthstone Publishing

14 Things Witches Hope Parents Never Find Out
David Benoit
ISBN 1-879366-76-2   2 audio tapes

The Revived Roman Empire and the Beast of the Apocalypse
N.W. Hutchings
ISBN 1-879366-31-2   150 pages

Why I Still Believe These Are the Last Days
ISBN 1-879366-38-X   250 pages

Footprints and the Stones of Time
Dr. Carl Baugh and Dr. Clifford Wilson
ISBN 1-879366-17-7   150 pages—Illustrated

Why So Many Churches?
N.W. Hutchings
ISBN 1-879366-28-2   200 pages

Petra In History and Prophecy
N.W. Hutchings
ISBN1-879366-11-8   160 pages—Illustrated

The Silver Kingdom: Iran in History and Prophecy
Mark Hitchcock
ISBN 1-879366-41-X   85 pages

What's Next?
Kenneth C. Hill
ISBN 1-879366-39-8   100 pages

Rapture and Resurrection
N.W. Hutchings
ISBN 1-879366-27-4   150 pages

Now Is the Dawning of the New Age New World Order
Dr. Dennis Cuddy
ISBN 1-879366-22-3   400 pages

For ordering information, call 1-800-580-2604